Who Said It Couldn't Be Done?

by
Denise Jones

Who Said It Couldn't Be Done?

ISBN: 978-1469912905

Library of Congress Control Number: 2010903783

Print in the United States of America

This paper is printed on acid- paper.

Who Said It Couldn't Be Done?

Editors:

Minnie Simpson

Marilyn Turner

All scripture quotations are taken from
The Authorized King James Version of The Word of God.

Who Said It Couldn't Be Done?

Diamond Photo courtesy of Israel Diamond
Institute…www.israelidiamond.co.il
& Cover Designed by Lynette K. Boswell PhD

Karen Feldman

Israel Diamond Institute

576 Fifth Avenue, Suite 301

New York, NY 10036

212-938-0888

KAREN@IDIUSA.NET

Ed Nightingale Photography

Iflash4u@msn.com

P.O. Box 1533

Calumet City, IL 60409

773-682-8510

CONTENTS

DEDICATION

This published work is dedicated to my mother, Annie Mae Freeman, whose extraordinary spiritual victory is the inspiration and launching pad, which began my own spiritual and personal healing. It is so amazing how it all worked out. Reminiscing on some of the things we have overcome causes a wide range of emotions to stir within my soul, all of which can be summed up in one word – GRATITUDE. Mother, I am so grateful; grateful for each snag we encountered, for each boulder we avoided, for each boulder we were incapable of avoiding, for each hard time we managed to overcome, and for all of the difficult situations we have survived. Wow! Look how far He has carried us…Mother, I love you.

To my spiritual Father in the Lord, Presiding Elder Donald L. Mosley, who has guided me in the Word and been there for me down through the years. I love you, appreciate the time, and care you put into every correction, chastisement, reproof and most of all, your love and gentleness toward me. You are the only father figure that I have ever known. Truly, you have filled a void in my life. Thank you for being the father I never had.

A special Thank you to Evangelist Christine Mosley, for her listening ear that heard my cries through all of my ups and downs. I can still hear you saying, "what about Jesus? What about Job? You ain't going through nothing!" You always encouraged me and offered your support when I needed you. I remember the day I finally allowed God to set me free. You came and hugged me so tightly then said, "Now stay free." With God's (and your) help, I endeavor to remain free. Thank you for everything.

Who Said It Couldn't Be Done?

To Elder Anthony Redmond and his lovely wife, Sister Donna Redmond (Baby): Thank you for your long-suffering and patience, right down to all the gray hairs for which I am personally responsible. You have been there for me through my difficulties. You have been a great source of strength. I can never forget your loyalty, the late night phone calls, the impromptu visits, the tears, the corrections, the rebukes and most of all your love.

To Jacquelyne Underwood and Bettye McGee: Thanks for being a shoulder during my school days. It's a very rare gift in life to have friends like you. Your support helped me succeed in achieving my education. For the first time in my life, I accomplished a goal worthwhile: my GED (It was God!). Jacquelyne, I remember when I called myself dropping out of school and throwing in the towel; you literally took me by the hand and led me all the way to the classroom and stayed with me the entire time. Who could ask for anything more? What a wonderful friend!

To Jean Johnson, Thank you for being a part of my life and for not turning your back on me when I was in my folly. You were always confident that I was going to make it. When I wanted to give up this fight, you told me to "fight on!" Your encouragement is always very timely and straight to the point.

Special thanks to Evangelist Patricia Harper for allowing God to use you in song. Your anointed vocal lead on *Stand Still Until His Will Is Clear* and *I Won't Doubt Your Love* continually inspires me to stand still and never doubt God's Love.

Special thanks to Evangelist Patricia Walker: For the last 25 years, I have never known you to change. You have always exhibited love to me and for me. Thank you for allowing God to use you on your vocal lead on *He Brought Joy Into My Life* and *I Surrender All.*

To Evangelist Regina L. Patillo, thank you for inviting me into your environment of God's True Holiness-Deliverance Ministries. One of the most important things I learned from you was to call my Annie Mother. I shall never forget your penetrating words to me, "I can't wait to see you preaching in lace and bows." Now my words to you are, All things are possible with GOD. Look how far we have come! I will always give thanks to JEHOVAH GOD for your support and unconditional love.

Who Said It Couldn't Be Done?

To everyone else who contributed to the publishing of this work . . . Thank you! Without all of you, my life would be a sad saga of tragedy. Your undying love and support have substantially contributed to my triumphant victory over mountains, which once seemed unconquerable.

REVIEWS

I congratulate and thank Denise for such a wonderful book. I think the book was very graphic and truthful. Most authors can't be that open and honest especially about themselves. The book showed how we cannot despise humble beginnings. It personally showed me just how faithful God is. I have never read a book that captivated my attention from the beginning of the book to the end of the book. The book was great.

Rene F. RN

***

After reading Denise's book, it only confirmed that people could change. It may not be an overnight transformation, but with a desire and an honest effort, it is possible; top that with trust in the Lord and you are guaranteed a change. Denise as a young child struggled with situations that an adult would have had great difficulty surviving. Then one day someone planted a seed, which gave her strength and acceptance of the Lord. With that she was off and running. I found the book easy to read; though quite graphic, it held my attention.

Anita B. RN

Who Said It Couldn't Be Done?

***

I have read many inspirational books but none compare to this. This book is very thought provoking. It reveals truthfulness…and most of all it is very edifying. I found it to be an easy read and recommended it to be a best seller. I am glad to have met Denise and her book gives hope to the one that feels hopeless. Thanks for sharing your miracle with me.

Yvonne T. RN

ACKNOWLEDGMENT

Teresa Collins thank you for all your hard work and assistance to make this book what it is today. I do not know what I would have done without your many years of labor. Teresa, you truly hung in there with me. You gave countless hours to working on my book. Your creative style of writing helped to develop the characters. Thank you for being dedicated and committed in making this book a reality.

Much Love,
Denise

FOREWARD

When I look back on how far Denise has come, it is truly *amazing*! Watching her overcome low self-esteem and blossom into the woman God is making her is absolutely God!

Imagine believing that it was impossible to achieve anything positive in life. Imagine thinking all you are good for is trying to prove to every man that you are a better man, when you are a *woman*. Imagine having a desire to go to school to become somebody, then reality tells you that you are incapable of staying focused long enough to learn anything. Then imagine that, *against all odds*, you overcome the impossible because God made *all* things possible. ***That is Denise.***

The life Denise was handed *seemed* unfair. The hand dealt to her *seemed* unreasonable, but when life goes a certain way, God always has a plan that can redefine your reality.

I affectionately call Denise "Onion" because I never saw a person eat so many onions! She kept telling me, "Onions are good for you." I would say, "Girl, that's ridiculous! All onions do is make your breath stink!" Well, onions didn't help Denise's natural eyes, but her spiritual eyes have definitely been enlightened. I affectionately call her "Mercedes" (and that's not her middle name) because I always knew behind the hard exterior of a Hummer she was indeed a Luxury Mercedes. Now I introduce to the world, my friend, the lady: Denise Jones.

Jacquelyne Underwood

PROLOGUE

PAIN

My earliest memory is of pain. I remember lying across my mother's lap on the living room sofa very early one Saturday morning. She was wasted from the night before. I could smell a creepy odor climbing out of her mouth. Years later, I learned it was the tart tinge of alcohol, forged with cigarette smoke camouflaged by Big Red chewing gum. Mother and her cheap wine had become one. The sultry lure of the liquid spirit had a bewitching way of overtaking her, causing her to believe she possessed incredible abilities. The prolific impulses came sharply; this time in the form of surgical powers.

Mother rummaged through the house searching for a sewing needle. She found the small piece of metal in one of the kitchen drawers, between a stack of folded grocery receipts and unopened junk mail. She burned the tip on the blue flame coming from our stove and then dipped it in rubbing alcohol. I can still remember the hissing noise that broke the uneasy silence as the hot steel collided with the cool liquid. She returned to her same position on the sofa and put my head back on her lap. She looked down at me and smiled, then pressed a small piece of ice against my earlobe to deaden my nerves, but it did not work. I cringed in blinding pain as my chilled skin cracked open under the sharp blow of that needle, then the slow sliding of it through my flesh. I screamed powerlessly at the top of my lungs and struggled pointlessly to free myself from the 'giant hand' possessing the 'evil dagger.'

Mother, still high and obviously oblivious to my mangled emotions and mounting agony, coldly immobilized my whirling head, then stabbed me a second time, ramming the 'dagger' clean through my other ear lobe. The nurturer who caressed my head upon her lap just moments earlier had grown fangs. My struggle was futile against her greedy assault. She seemed amused, pleased even, at the escalating level of my terror. I looked up at her again, but this time in stark confusion; she was still smiling, and then she started laughing. Her wicked laughter taunted my dizzy head, which was still pinned to her hard, collaborating knee. I shivered in fear; my teeth chattered. A quiet stream of blood flowed from my nose but no tears would follow. Suddenly I was more afraid than I had ever been, especially of my mother's hand. Her hand had frightened me many times before; it had always been harsh, but that day it was harsher, colder, than I had ever seen it. Her hand seemed hungry somehow; salivating as if it wanted to kill me and swallow me whole. I felt a need to keep my mother's hand back, but her teeth were still showing and that frightened me. I shut my eyes tightly, took in a deep breath…and screamed some more. At three years old, that was all I could do.

I suppose that ear piercing was an omen of the pattern of my early life: hurt and abuse often inflicted by my mother, and me unable to do anything about it. I became an unread paperback in my mother's hand: she was bending me backward as if she were interested in the pages of my life, but line after line went unread. My preface, my forward, my contents, each chapter were all but mere shadows in her hand; jumbled messages of oddly constructed paragraphs of meaninglessness. She could not decipher the words of the script. They were left dangling on the pages of chance. I didn't understand why she did not respond to the many times I reached for her. My love that I offered unconditionally, the smile upon my face that lit whatever room she entered, the interest I took in her walk, her smell, the sound of her voice, even her slap and the pain that it caused on the side of my face. I was attentive to every line she wrote, but my life was not translated. The late nights I stayed awake listening for her keys to jingle in the door, or to hear her cowboy boots scrape across the floor; the noise I made, the tears I cried and the tears I carried in my heart; the trouble I started, the fights I had, the mistakes I made; nothing I did seemed to matter. My emotional state went undetected, like an unsolved mystery.

ANNIE MAE

1

PRAYER CHANGES THINGS

It is something of a miracle that I was even born. Back when my mother, Annie Mae Jones, was only eight years old, she and a friend decided to go bike riding through the neighborhood. Suddenly the car struck forty-eight pound Annie Mae, she was thrown from the bike and flung haphazardly into the air. The driver of the car panicked and swerved all over the street. When Annie Mae smashed to the ground, the massive car made a remarkable finish as well. Its tremendous front wheel plopped down for the last time, and Annie Mae didn't move; she didn't do anything, not even blink. A growing pool of blood oozed from beneath the resting wheel. Everyone thought Annie Mae was dead. She was so small that the huge tire seemed to cover her entire body, though it rested only on her stomach. Neighbors from all around gathered, squinting at the alarming sight as they watched the firefighters pry poor Annie Mae from beneath that killer wheel.

Matted in clunks of blood and dirt, lifeless Annie Mae was rushed by ambulance to Mary Thompson Hospital, where it was determined that she was hemorrhaging. The Hospital Director signed proxy for the surgery required to stop the bleeding. When Annie Mae's parents arrived, they were told that, given the extent of Annie Mae's injuries, the Director's quick action probably saved Annie Mae's life. She was losing so much blood that she would have certainly died if they had waited for her parents to arrive.

After twenty-three hours of pacing back and forth in the waiting room, Nathaniel and Annie Belle Jones were finally able to breathe a sigh of relief when the doctor told them that the surgery was successful and all signs of hemorrhaging had ceased. However, their short spurt of jubilation fizzled fast as the doctor continued his report. "We were able to stop the hemorrhaging, but it still doesn't look good. Annie Mae is in a coma."

Grandmother screamed out in agony and grabbed her chest, falling back clumsily into Grandfather. He caught her before she hit the floor and helped her to a nearby chair. The doctor brought Grandmother a cup of water and when she was able to compose herself, he delivered the worst part of the report. "Annie Mae's reproductive organs were irreversibly damaged by the accident, which means she will never be able to bear children."

"Oh my God. Lord Jesus! Oh my Sweet Jesus!!" Grandmother screamed out over and over, clutching her chest again. The doctor assured them that he and the rest of the hospital staff would do everything in their power to help Annie Mae recover, then he left them to themselves.

What followed could probably be noted as the first move of God in my life, or what would later become my life. God used a powerful, praying woman of deep spiritual faith: Evangelist Mattie B. Poole. Evangelist Poole was a regular visitor at Mary Thompson Hospital in those days. Often this Woman of God would march down the halls of the huge building, stopping at the bedside of patients, known and unknown, to dispense her straightforward knowledge of God's Word, His loving care and healing power. Evangelist Poole knew that the Lord had given her the gift of healing, so her ministry largely involved prayer and the "laying on of hands" on the sick to aid their recovery.

During one of Evangelist Poole's visits, she entered little Annie Mae's room and marveled at the small, lifeless child lying there. Slowly she stretched for her hands, placing them firmly on the comatose child as my grandparents looked on silently. "Heavenly Father, in Jesus' Name," Evangelist Poole whispered, "bring this peculiar child back to life. Awaken her from this unusual sleep; this unnatural, comatose state. Grant this precious and innocent child an opportunity to tread the path that You have marked and chosen for her feet to travel. And Father, in Jesus' Name, I humbly ask that You restore ten-fold, thirty-fold, sixty-fold, and even one hundred-fold, health and strength so that she may accomplish and complete her destined purpose; the purpose You have ordained for her life, even before this precious child was born. Father, in the Wonderful Name of Your Darling Son, Christ Jesus, I ask you to restore this child's reproductive organs. Allow her womb to be fertile, that she may bear children, even children that will bring Thy Name glory and honor, both male and female alike in Jesus' Name."

Grandmother sat up straight in the chair and leaned forward as she witnessed Annie Mae's eyelids begin to twitch for the first time since she was pulled from beneath the car. As Evangelist Poole continued praying, Annie Mae's parents watched in amazement as Annie Mae began wiggling beneath the white cotton sheets. By the time Evangelist Poole concluded her prayer, Annie Mae was completely out of the coma.

Astonished, Grandmother and Grandfather looked at each other, then back at Annie Mae, unable to find words to express their amazement as well as their gratitude. Fully conscious and responsive now, Annie Mae questioned her whereabouts and expressed a desire for some of

Grandmother's red beans and rice. Grandmother was smiling as she turned around to thank Evangelist Poole for allowing God to use her in such a mighty way, but she was nowhere to be found.

2

LOSS OF INNOCENCE

Annie Mae had a mind of her own. She knew what she was doing and believed that George was in love with her. Why else would he let her help him build his bombs? George and Annie had been next-door neighbors for nearly six years and had become good friends. They, along with some of the other children in the neighborhood, often played games together. Catch a Girl, Get a Girl was one of the neighborhood favorites, as well as Hide-and-Seek and Spin the Bottle.

George always chased after Annie Mae when they played Catch a Girl, Get a Girl, and when they played Hide-and-Seek, he would always manage to hide in the same place as Annie Mae. George couldn't control Spin the Bottle, but if he could, I imagine that bottle would have landed on Annie Mae every time.

One day during a game of Hide-and-Seek, Annie Mae was hiding in the gangway behind the building where they lived at 16th and Ridgeway on the West Side of Chicago. George walked up behind her and began pressing his body against hers, the way he always did. Annie Mae leaned on George and let her head fall backward until it rested on his chest. Forcefully, he thrust his pelvis forward and Annie Mae got caught up in the moment, enjoying the liberty of grinding back on George. Silently the two stood there, twelve and thirteen years of age, grinding away. When they heard footsteps approaching, they pushed apart in a hurry; Annie Mae ran her way and George ran his.

Some weeks later, Grandmother made pancakes for breakfast, but did not realize she was out of syrup until she was finished. "Annie Mae, go across the hall to Miss Smith's apartment and ask if they have any syrup, if you don't mind sweetheart; and ask her if she wants some of these cakes I flipped up. Tell her it's a good batch, stacked tall."

Annie knocked on the door and waited for someone to answer. She hoped to see George, but her growling stomach yearned more to see the bottle of syrup and feel the warm hotcakes slide down her throat. To her delight, George did answer. "Hey George," Annie said, while brushing past him and walking right into the house, heading straight toward the kitchen.

"I know your big old gorilla-head, Martian-head-self didn't just push past me and walk up in my momma house. Did I invite you in?" George said smiling, glad to see Annie.

"No," said Annie while sucking her teeth, "but you ain't never invited me in before. I always have to push my way up in here, 'cause you're always acting like a security guard, guarding that door. You barely even open it up, standing there talking to me through that little, bitty old crack. I can hardly see you. You might as well open it up, cuz I be in here anyway. Even when y'all ain't home, I be in here. I be in the living room watching y'alls TV and eating up y'alls food," Annie said laughing, while lightly muffing George on the side of his head. "My momma sent me over here to see if your mother will let us borrow some syrup. She made a big batch of pancakes, but we need some syrup. Y'all got some?"

"We probably do, but you know how my momma is. We can't let nobody borrow nothing unless she's home and she's not here right now," he said.

"Okay, I guess I'll go then. We don't need your nasty old syrup anyway. Besides, my momma's pancakes taste better with jelly. They good like that too, huh? Have you ever had them like that, George?"

"Yeah, I eat them like that all the time," said George. "I don't even like syrup. I always put jelly on mine, and I like it on my sausage too. I make sandwiches out of my pancakes, eggs and sausage. I bet you never thought of doing that, have you smarty pants?"

Annie rolled her eyes, ignoring George's teasing and asked, "You coming outside later?"

"I should," said George, "once my momma gets home. But after you eat, why don't you come back over?"

Annie smiled at the invitation, "Okay, as long as you open the door, with your big Martian-head, so I don't have to be squeezing through that tiny little crack any more."

George smiled. "Alright, I'll see you when you get back, and hurry up, big head." He closed the door and Annie went back to her apartment across the hall.

"Momma, George said his mother wasn't home so he couldn't lend nothing out. Looks like we'll be having jelly on our pancakes today." Grandmother heard but didn't respond; she simply flipped the last few pancakes while softly singing *Lord, Don't Move My Mountain.*

Annie was eager to dig into the fluffy pancakes. Almost before her mother finished setting her plate down, she grabbed her knife and began spreading grape jelly all over them. Then she made a sandwich with her sausage and cheesy eggs, the way George said he did. When she finished eating, she sped through her chores and asked to go outside to play. Grandmother said it was fine, as long as she stayed in the neighborhood and didn't stay gone too long. Before leaving the house, Annie Mae changed her clothes, putting on her favorite plaid dress with the white collar and the two big pockets in the front. She liked that dress because it was wide and comfortable. She could run fast in it, which helped her get away when they played Catch a Girl, Get A Girl. She didn't bother putting on socks; she just slipped on her white Converse tennis shoes. They were a little old, but they still fit and were in good shape. Annie then combed her hair in three ponytails, leaving a big bang in the front. Everyone always said how cute she looked with bangs, so she always wore them.

After saying goodbye to Grandmother, Annie made lots of noise as she stomped down the stairs from their third-floor apartment. She went down to the second floor and sat for a minute, acting like she was tying her shoe before stealthily tiptoeing back up the stairs and tapping lightly on George's door. This time when George answered, he opened the door wide and was about to yell, "COME ON IN," but Annie Mae quickly put her hand over his mouth and hurried inside, looking back at her apartment door to make sure nobody was watching. She quietly closed

George's door behind herself and pulled George into the living room.

"Girl, what is wrong with you?" George said.

"Fool!" she whispered. "Is you crazy? I don't want my mother to know I'm in here. I asked her could I go *outside*, not could I be in here with you." They both started laughing.

"Come on, Annie," George said. "Let's go in my room, so I can show you something." Sure enough, it was another bomb. She was always intrigued with George's inventions. It amazed and impressed her that he could build bombs that actually exploded. He had set the hallway of their apartment building on fire many times experimenting with them, but it never got too serious; they were always able to put the flames out themselves before any damage was done.

"Wow, George," Annic Mae said, looking at George's latest invention. "How do you know how to build bombs like that?"

"I don't know," he said. "I just do. I like making stuff. I experiment with things, put some wires together, and BOOM!" Startled by George's loud outburst, Annie Mae jumped.

"Why did you jump?" he asked, as he moved away from the dresser and walked over to the edge of his bed where she was sitting. He moved in on Annie Mae as much as he could, until his legs were straddling hers. Gently he placed his hands on her shoulder and leaned her backward until she was lying down on his bed. Placing his body on top of hers, he began slowly parting her legs with his knee.

"So, why you so jumpy?" he repeated, but in a quieter tone as he gently kissed her lips. Annie loved the way George's lips felt, because they were full and soft.

"Why you gotta make so much noise? You are too loud," she said. "Anyway, what time is your mother coming back?" George got silent. *Why she got to go and mention my mother?* he thought. *She has to know I'm trying to get me some.* Thoughts began to race through George's mind. He was upset that Annie tried to ruin the mood, but reality was beginning to set in. *What if we get caught? What if I get her pregnant? I can't be no daddy. Maybe I should just get up and stop fooling with this girl.* However, those rational thoughts came and went. Overwhelmed by his teenage hormones, George promptly forgot about his what ifs and maybes and made another move.

Who Said It Couldn't Be Done?

"Shhhh," he whispered in her ear. "Be quiet Annie Mae, with your pretty self. You know, I really like you Annie Mae, I really do. You're the only girl for me."

Annie Mae, like George, was having conflicting feelings as well. His sweet words were blinding her. She felt queasy in her stomach and light-headed, like when you climb up a big hill then run down real fast. She was inebriated by George's sweetness. *Wow, I really like you too, George,* is what Annie thought, but she kept her thoughts to herself. Although she had wonderful feelings toward George, she was also having second thoughts about their passionate moment and was definitely uncomfortable about going all the way. *Yeah, he's cute and all, and we kissed and grinded before*, she thought to herself, *but having sex? Naw, I'm not doing that. Only a nasty girl would be sittin' up here having sex with boys.* Annie and some of the other girls in the neighborhood had talked about it, but she never envisioned she would be in a situation like this. *I ain't no nasty girl*, she said to herself. *What if we do it and he tells all his friends? Everybody will know we did it and they'll be calling me nasty. And I ain't nasty.*

Annie's heart raced as she continued to contemplate the situation in her mind. *I'm scared*, she thought. *What if this is all he wants? Besides, I don't know what to do. I never did it before, and I am afraid to do it. Will he still like me if I say no? Will he still play with me? Will he still let me help him with his bombs?*

Annie did not know how to express all that she was feeling to George, and she did not want to hurt his feelings or lose him, so she laid there and allowed him to part her legs more. Besides, her concerns did not seem to be as important as the mounting pleasure she felt lying beneath George's body. They laid there another moment, enjoying the warmth that came from being so close. Staring into each other's eyes each thought and wondered about the possibilities of what could happen. As the air thickened in the room, Annie could not resist George's touch, nor did she want to. George continued kissing Annie's lips and her strength seemed to melt away with each juvenile press of his mouth against hers. She parted her watering lips a little more, to allow his tongue to slide easily inside. Caught in the heat of the moment, George began to sweat but Annie did not mind. She enjoyed their closeness. She took her hands and placed them on his damp back, then hesitantly slid them downward until they rested below his waist. Delicate parts of her body were awakening for the very first time. Good, tingly feelings were jumping inside her. These were feelings that only George had made her feel. *I must love George*, Annie thought. *I wouldn't feel this way if I didn't.* Annie noticed George reacting to her body and could tell he felt the same way. At that moment, all Annie knew was that she wanted George. However, at a naive twelve years of age, Annie was not capable of comprehending the door she was about to open.

George continued pressing against Annie more and more until finally he stood up, unzipped his pants, and drew his penis into full view. Annie's eyes widened and her heart pounded frantically as she quickly turned her head to avoid looking at it. *Oh no*, she said to herself. *I'm scared! Look at that thing! He's not touching me with that ugly thing. No way! What am I doing? No, no! Don't do it; don't do it, Annie Mae, don't do it. No, no, no! Don't do it, don't do it....*

When George and Annie's moment of foolish, adolescent indulgence ended, so did their friendship. George did not feel the same way Annie did after all. As Annie Mae laid on the bed staring at George, it was obvious that he was visibly avoiding all eye contact with her. However, she did observe him covertly taking pleasure in what seemed to be a long-awaited victory. She saw him smiling smugly as he dragged the zipper of his pants back up the track, eyeing her out of the corner of his eye then proudly swaggering back over to the dresser to toy with his bomb. Annie did not like that. It made her feel used and rejected, the same way her daddy made her feel. She closed her eyes as the memories began to flood her mind...

Every summer Annie and Mable, Annie Mae's older sister, would spend many weekends with their biological father. Mable always slept in the bed with their father while a pallet was prepared on the floor for Annie. Feeling jealous, Annie always begged and pleaded to sleep with her father.

"Please, Daddy, please. Can I sleep with you tonight?"

"Naw, not tonight baby girl; maybe next time," he would say, while glancing over at Mable. Mable would never respond to him or Annie, but she always listened intently.

Finally, on one of their visits, Annie's wish came true. Mable was instructed to take the pallet and give Annie the bed. Seven year old Annie was so excited she could hardly wait. Attempting to taunt Mable, Annie began to bounce up and down on the bed while singing, "I'm gonna sleep with Daddy, I'm gonna sleep with Daddy!" Mable didn't appear to be moved by Annie's foolishness. She just continued watching television.

Annie rushed through her bath, put on her nightgown and jumped into bed. "Come on, Daddy!" she exclaimed. "When are you coming to bed?"

"In a little bit, baby girl, in a little bit," he slurred, while resting one hand on his private part and turning up the bottle of cheap wine with the other. Their father lingered in the living room a long while, staring blankly at the television and drinking his wine, before he finally swaggered into the bedroom. Annie was already asleep, but her peaceful state was abruptly halted by a roving intruder: her father's big hands fondling her little body.

"Oh no," Annie gasped. "Stop, Daddy, don't," she said, trying to push his hand away.

"Ssssh," he whispered. "Daddy loves his baby girl," he said, as he took her hand and began to rub it up and down on his penis. "You're growing up now, turning out to be real pretty. Feel how much Daddy loves his baby? Hush now, you don't want to wake your sister."

Lying three feet away on a pallet on the floor, Mable was wide-awake and listening to every word, tears silently rolling down her cheeks.

Who Said It Couldn't Be Done?

The next morning was somber; guilt and shame filled the tiny apartment. Shirtless, their father sat at the breakfast table, drinking coffee and staring out the window. After washing their faces, the girls took their seats around the table. "Hey there, how's Daddy's two little princesses?" *their father asked, trying to perk things up a bit. Neither of them responded. Neither could bear to look at him. Mable was angry and didn't mind showing it, but Annie was confused.*

It's my fault. I made Daddy mad, *Annie Mae thought*. I'm a bad girl. Does he do that to Mable too? Why did I make him let me sleep with him? Daddy must hate me. I'm afraid of Daddy. I want my mommy. *These were the thoughts and questions bombarding Annie Mae's mind, but she kept her thoughts and feelings inside.*

He took his hand and stroked his chest a few times, and then asked Mable to fix him some breakfast. After they ate, he took them home. "Alright now, y'all give Daddy a big hug. Be good now. I'll see y'all next weekend. And here you go, Annie, for being Daddy's big girl." *He handed her fifty cents and gave Mable a dollar bill.*

From that point on, Annie hated going to visit her father, but her mother forced her to go, unaware of the abuse that was taking place. Thus, the cycle of incest continued.

*   *   *

Now, feeling used and confused once again, Annie smacked her lips and jumped up from the bed. "Forget you then, George. I'm fixin' to go," she snapped. Slowly she began straightening her clothes and smoothing her hair down, hoping that George would look up and ask her to stay, but George never took his eyes off of that silly bomb. Angry now, Annie pranced out of the bedroom and proceeded through the living room toward the front door. Carefully she cracked the door and peeped into the hallway, to see if the coast was clear. When she saw it was safe, she tiptoed down the stairs to the second floor landing, then turned around and stomped back up the stairs, deliberately making lots of noise in case her mother was listening from the front room.

3

THE CONVERSATION

"Psst! Baby girl, don't you hear me talking to you? Say, young lady. Hey gal, you pregnant, huh? Ain't you? Why you just standing there? Why you standing out there in that hot morning sun, baking like that?" In the doorway of the storefront church directly in front of where Annie Mae was standing, stood a middle-aged woman, somewhat wide-hipped with graying temples. She had not asked for a conversation; she had gone outside to play, but it was still a bit early and none of her friends was outside yet. As she waited, she roamed around the neighborhood, block after block, with a large stick in her hand, letting her imagination flow. First, she dragged the stick leisurely on the ground, and then she pretended it was a cane, and finally she used it as a weed whacker, swinging at any tall grass and shrubbery that crossed her path.

"That baby ain't even made it into the world yet and you already doing something you ain't got no business doing. Come on gal; get yourself out that sun before both you and that baby turn into a pan of fresh-baked apple fritters. Come sit up here with me on this porch where it's a little bit cooler. I'll go fetch you some ice water. Don't be afraid; come here gal." The big metal church door was

25

propped open with a steel-framed folding chair the woman had lodged beneath the doorknob. Resting beside her was a large, silver boiling pot. It appeared that pot had boiled many meals in its day; Annie spotted all of the dents and burn spots clearly from the sidewalk where she stood, pretending not to mind the woman or the old pot.

The woman sat down next to the pot and began snapping green beans. The blade of the paring knife flickered from the glare of the morning sun every time she snipped a tip. After a moment, the woman called to Annie once more. "Young lady, come here, baby; I'm not going to hurt you." Annie still did not budge, she just stood there, hard as a rock on the sweating sidewalk, staring straight ahead, wondering about what the woman said.

Why would she say that? How could she know? Is it true? Am I really pregnant? I'm not showing or nothing. Huh, ain't no baby inside me.

Like lint, Annie brushed the woman off and got back to her journey, however the woman was unrelenting. As Annie walked down the street away from the church porch, the woman continued calling after her. "Young lady," she cried, "you're very pretty; you're a pretty lil' thang. You're going to have lots of lady friends around you, but you can't trust any of them. You hear me, gal?

You can't trust none of them. They are going to be jealous of you. You watch yourself, you hear me? Hey, young lady! I'm trying to tell you something! Get yourself back here. Young lady!"

Annie was nearly two blocks away, but the woman's unsettling words still rang in her ears, as though they were standing face to face. When the woman stood to her feet, she raised the hand holding the paring knife over her brow to block the glare of the sun as she observed Annie Mae vanishing in the growing distance. Her eyes watered as she wiped her other hand on her stained apron. Annie Mae was gone; she never answered the woman and never looked back.

When Annie Mae finally made it home, she reflected on her adventure. She could not shake the conversation from her mind. She knew she had missed some of her periods, but she didn't look pregnant. She wasn't showing at all. Besides, her parents told her that she could not have any children.

4

COMING OF AGE

Several months had passed and Annie Mae had forgotten about her encounter with the woman on the church porch. It was Aunt Rosa Mae's wedding day and Grandmother was running around trying to hurry everyone out to the car. "Y'all gals hurry up," her mother yelled. "You know we have got to be at the church. I don't want to be late. Rosa Mae will never let me live it down, coming up in there late, with you two gals hanging on my arm. Oooh, Rosa Mae will act a fool, y'all know how she is. I'll never hear the end of it, so come on now, before I leave both of you sitting right here!"

"Well leave then," Mable said, mumbling under her breath. Annie and Mable were rushing around their room trying to get ready. Mable kept sassing back as her mother continued hurrying them. "We coming. Why you fussing so much? We can't get ready with you always stopping us, talking to us and yelling, telling us to get ready, get ready, get ready. That's what we doing. Leave us alone!"

Grandmother came into the room. "Mable, if you don't shut your mouth, girl …" Annie could not stand the way Mable sassed back at their mother, but that's how Mable was: no one could control her. You couldn't tell her

28

a thing. She had an answer for everybody and she knew *every*thing. She was always getting in trouble with the teachers at school for talking back, and in their neighborhood, she was known as Big Mouth Mable.

Hurriedly, Annie was trying to get herself ready, but the dress she planned to wear to the wedding no longer fit. Most of her clothes had gotten tight, so she wore the same few tops over and over. Finally, she put on a skirt and a blouse and left the blouse outside of her skirt. Looking over herself one last time in the mirror, she smoothed down her bangs, then grabbed her sweater and ran out to the car.

Grandmother arrived at the church in plenty of time and the ceremony went well. At the reception, Aunt Rosa Mae's husband kept staring at Annie Mae. She did not know why he was looking at her but it was awkward, as if he was trying to figure something out. Finally, he leaned over and nudged Aunt Rosa Mae, then whispered something in her ear. Aunt Rosa Mae immediately turned to Annie and began staring as well. Just then, Grandmother came and informed Annie and Mable she had arranged for them to be taken home, so the adults could get on with the party.

When they arrived home, Annie and Mable decided to lie down and take a nap. A few hours later, their mother arrived home and marched right into the bedroom where Mable and Annie Mae were napping. "Annie Mae! Get yo' fast tail up, gal. Is you pregnant? You better not be cuz if you pregnant, you going right down there to the Audy Home with all them other fast-tail gals. Who you been lettin' feel up under your clothes? Stand up! Let me see your stomach!"

Still groggy from her nap, Annie Mae sat up in bed and rubbed her eyes. While she was trying to come into a coherent state and decipher what all the yelling was about, her mother took the back of her hand and struck Annie Mae across the face. "I told you to stand up, gal!" Grandmother snapped. "Let me look at your stomach. Is you pregnant?"

"Yeah!" teary-eyed Annie shouted as she jumped out of the bed, raising up her blouse and pulling her skirt below her belly. Grandmother struck her again across the face. "What is wrong with you, Annie Mae? How can you be pregnant? How could you embarrass this family like this? How could you be so stupid? You know better than this. Who you been letting feel up under your clothes? It bet not be that nappy-headed George. That boy ain't sniffin' around but for one thang. He been with every girl in this neighborhood, and here you is, silly like all the rest of them dumb girls. Now tell me, cuz it bet not be him!"

Who Said It Couldn't Be Done?

Mable could not sleep amid all the commotion. As she sat up and looked around, trying to take in all that was going on around her, Grandmother snatched Mable out of the bed and began thrashing her heartlessly with Grandfather's good leather belt. "It's your fault," Grandmother screamed. "It's your fault! You knew this girl was pregnant. Why didn't you tell me?" Grandmother's temper escalated more and more until she didn't even notice that all the buttons on her dress had burst open. Her eyes were stretched wide, like they were ready to pop out of her skull; her teeth gnashed together; sweat ran down her forehead and covered her face and her hair sweated back and charged in all directions. Grandmother was swinging Grandfather's belt so wildly she could have beaten off a bear. All Mable could do was bare the whipping, so she balled up in a knot on the floor and covered her face with both arms. For the first time in her life, Mable had nothing to say.

"Ahhhhh," Annie screamed over and over. "Ahhhh, I don't care. Do what you wanna do! I don't give a care." Annie was falling apart. So many thoughts were rushing through her mind; there was so much she needed to say. *I try to be good. I'm a good girl, I really am. I'm not nasty, I made a mistake. Don't be mad at me. Please don't be mad.*

Who Said It Couldn't Be Done?

I'm sorry. I'm scared. What am I going to do? I don't know what to do. Please stop yelling at me and don't hit Mable no more! Why you saying it's her fault? It's not her fault. Stop saying you gonna put me out. I don't wanna go, I want you to hold me and tell me it's gonna be okay. Tell me; please tell me its okay. Please don't hate me.

Those were Annie Mae's thoughts, but not what came out of her mouth. She screamed at her mother at the top of her lungs, "I don't care what you say, do what you wanna do! I don't care no more!" Her mother was shocked. She had never seen Annie this angry before. Annie Mae had never talked back, had an outburst, or hardly given her parents any trouble at all. Startled by Annie Mae's sharp reply, her mother dropped her father's belt, wiped her brow with the top of her forearm and stood there quietly. By now, everybody had made it back home and began gathering into the bedroom. Everybody was screaming at everybody. No one knew what was going on or what caused all the chaos, but it was mad bedlam at 16th and Ridgeway that night. Finally, her Grandfather grabbed Grandmother and tried to calm her down. Annie Mae fell to the floor, crying uncontrollably and rocking back and forth.

Mable regained the use of her vocals and defended her honor. She stood to her feet and let Grandmother have it. "Why is you beating me?" she shouted. "Your precious Annie is the one with the big stomach, but you beat me. You just gotta blame me for everything. I didn't lay up there and have sex with that nasty boy; Annie did that so beat her! Beat your baby, but don't touch me. I don't have nothing to do with it. I don't be with Annie. How am I supposed to know she's somewhere laying down letting some stupid boy do it with her? I always knew you loved her better than me anyway. All y'all treat her better than you treat me. I can't stand y'all!" Grandmother did nothing. "Yeah, I thought so," Mable said. "That's why I hate y'all. Good for her," she said, looking spitefully at Annie. "I'm glad she's pregnant." Mable looked at Grandmother, then at each person silently observing her tirade, and lastly at Annie Mae. With nothing left to say, she turned and pushed her way out of the room.

The next morning things were calm, but thick tension filled the house. It was evident that another angry outburst was standing nearby, awaiting the opportunity to launch another full-fledged attack. The horrible events of the previous evening had turned Annie Mae's passionate heart cold. She could not handle all the pressure that her actions brought upon the family and could not push past all of the unkind things Grandmother had said. Annie Mae was always a sensitive child, everyone knew it, and so they always spoke kindly to her. No one knew about all the hurt and abuse Annie Mae kept hidden deep inside her. The incestuous molestation by her father and being used and rejected by George had created a black hole inside her, wide and deep. Thirteen year old Annie Mae abandoned her hopes and dreams of a joyful, happy future and climbed inside that hole, where she would dwell many years, lost and in great pain.

Annie Mae never saw George again, except from her bedroom window, but George did not seem to mind. Annie Mae's heart ached as she watched him chasing all the other girls in the neighborhood, and spending more and more time with her sister, Mable. Mable and George were becoming good friends. George enjoyed grabbing and touching Mable in the same way he had touched Annie; and as rumors did tell, the two were soon the neighborhood's next piece of raunchy gossip.

Annie Mae was a prisoner, doing hard time in the confines of her bedroom, exercising freedom only for meals, bathroom privileges and doctor visits. She could not endure her embarrassing shame. Further and further she sank, disappearing into a cavity of deep depression, isolation and acute loneliness, nurturing hatred for her world and everyone in it, especially Mable.

Eventually George was sent away to live with relatives in another state. The day before he left, Annie Mae watched him from her window all day long. Though George knew she was in the window, he never looked up. Annie missed playing with all her friends, but she especially missed George. She missed playing Hide-and-Seek and Catch a Girl, Get a Girl. She wanted so much to be with him. She missed his touch, his body, his kiss. She missed watching him build his bombs while they talked about their future and what they wanted to be when they grew up. Oooh, what Annie wouldn't give to be with George once again!

Feeling lost and in total despair, Annie placed both hands on the window, laid her face against them and began to cry. "Oh George," she whispered, "what about me?" She wanted George to catch her and kiss her again, remembering their very first time. They were playing a game of Catch a Girl, Get a Girl. The usual group was there.

"Uh, I got you," George said to Annie, as he seized her and pulled her close to him. "Now gimmie my kiss."

"No," Annie said, turning her head back and forth teasingly. "I ain't giving you nothing," she said, while trying to pull away, but his grip was strong.

"Uh-uh Annie, I caught you fair and square," George said, with a hint of agitation in his voice. Then he let her go and started singing the song, "I Got You" by Joe Tex.

"You thought I couldn't get you, uh-huh huh. But I got you, uh-huh huh. You thought I couldn't get you, uh-huh huh. But I got you, uh-huh huh…"

Annie Mae looked down from the window in time to see George disappear into the gangway with one of the neighborhood girls. Annie Mae pressed hard and angrily against her swelling stomach, "I hate this baby. Do you hear me, you stupid, nasty thing? I hate you!" Crying harder now, she walked to the closet and removed a hanger. She slid the cardboard rod from between the wire hinges, and then threw the hanger to the floor, walking back toward the window. A rapid flow of tears streamed down her face as she stared blankly out of the window, as if the sidewalk beneath was a distant land, though it was just three stories below. After a few minutes, she walked over to her bedroom door and jammed it shut, so no one could enter, then she laid in the bed and silently cried herself to sleep.

When Annie awakened an hour later, she still could not shake her thoughts of George and how he had used and abandoned her. Being pregnant was overwhelming enough, but the father of her child didn't want anything to do with her, let alone the child she was carrying. She couldn't take the pressure anymore. Annie turned from her side to lie flat on her back and removed her panties. She raised her left leg, the way the doctor did when he examined her, then the right leg and slid the cardboard stick inside her vagina. Then she breathed in deeply and rammed it as hard as she could.

At age thirteen, when most young girls are just beginning to blossom into womanhood, Annie Mae was pregnant with me.

*   *   *

"That girl ain't old enough to be bringing up nobody's baby!" Grandmother protested adamantly. "But I know what to do." Grandmother began to concoct various potions and elixirs for Annie to drink, that supposedly would bring on premature labor. For several months, Grandmother brewed her liquid cure-alls and presented them to Annie. "Here, Annie, drink this; it will make you feel better." Each time it was the same story.

"Eww, that stinks," Annie would say. "What is it?"

"Don't worry about all that," Grandmother would snap back. "Just drink it, it's good for you. It's medicine. Something that'll fix everything and put things back on track, the way they supposed to be. Now drink up!"

Annie would drink Grandmother's concoctions, each time, just a few moments after the first sip, the elixir would do a wild dance in her belly and find itself leaping out of her stomach, making its way through her esophagus to dance all over the floor in front of her. All of Grandmother's intentions were to no avail. On November 10, 1960 (a full week overdue), at Rush Presbyterian Hospital, thirteen year old Annie Mae Jones gave birth to her first-born child: a curly-topped, bright-eyed baby girl weighing eight pounds and seven ounces. She named her Denise Jones.

NIECY BONE

5

BITTER-SWEET HOME

The family was in pandemonium. Everyone was battling over who would raise me. When the smoke cleared, I became the prize possession of my grandparents on my mother's side and went to live in their home, along with my mother and my Aunt Mable. My family often recounts stories about my life as an infant. I have heard many times how I was only three months old when my mother first snuck out of the house and left me home alone. I guess my mother thought that since Aunt Mable was in the house, Aunt Mable would be moved with compassion and watch me until she returned. However, Aunt Mable definitely was not going to be sitting around holding a baby and making goo-goo eyes all day long. I was not <u>her</u> baby. She had already made plans to be with her friends and was in the process of getting ready to meet them. My mother actually knew this, but to justify her negligence she created elaborate excuses in her mind.

One particular time, when mother snuck out and left me for my aunt to care for, Aunt Mable laced my bottle of milk with some type of sleeping pill and flew out the door. I've been told that the sleeping pill caused me to sleep all that night and half the following day. Looking back, death has been stalking me since before I was born.

It grieved Grandmother to see how ruthless her precious Annie Mae had become. Often Grandmother talked to her, or rather yelled at her, and tried to force her to take care of me. "Annie, go in there and get that baby! Don't you hear her doing all that hollering? Go change her diaper, gal! Give her a bottle and burp her!" But as usual, my mother ignored Grandmother's demands and sauntered on out the door. Mother was too busy chasing boys. There was always some guy waiting outside to see my mother. They were always telling her how cute she was, which she loved to hear, so it wasn't long before her belly was poking out again. She had one baby after another until there were five of us. My brother, Stanley, was born in 1961 – only a year after me. My sister Regina was born in 1963, and Benesse was born shortly after in 1964. Then Linzie came along in 1968. It was always the same story: the babies kept coming and the fathers kept going. There were four fathers in all and none of them stayed around. And neither did our mother.

Nevertheless, life with my grandparents was good. Their marriage was common law, but I was lavished with generous helpings of love from them both. They spoiled me rotten. Grandfather smothered me with attention, and I just soaked it up! I remember when I was four years old, I would always look out of the window and wait for my grandfather to come home from work. Excitedly I would run outside barefooted to meet him. One day all the excitement got the best of me. As usual, I ran outside barefooted with my wide grin leading the way, only this time I tripped over an old pipe that was in my path and split my ankle open all the way to the bone. Blood gushed out all over the ground and covered the rusty pipe. Grandfather jumped out of his car, lifted me from the ground and rushed me around the corner to the neighborhood doctor. I wasn't afraid until I heard the doctor say I needed eight stitches. I wasn't sure what stitches were, but they sounded scary. When the doctor came in with a needle, I immediately remembered the painful ear piercing forced upon me by my mother. I looked at Grandfather, eyes wide, and let out my loudest scream.

It turned out not to be so bad after all. The doctor and Grandfather were very patient and gentle with me, not like my mother when she stabbed me in my earlobes. When the doctor finished his delicate work, Grandfather took me for ice cream, hoping that French vanilla stuffed in a waffle cone would cheer his little darling up, and it did!

Grandmother was also very kind to me. She always said that out of all of my siblings, I was her baby. She was a strong, loving influence in my life, though she wasn't as affectionate as Grandfather. She rarely hugged or kissed me, it just wasn't her way. Her role, however, was very significant in my life. Grandmother taught me how to be responsible and care for a home. It was Grandmother who bought my first Easy Bake Oven and taught me how to use it. Often we would make Easy Bake cakes and cornbread together. Grandmother was a wonderful cook. I still have fond memories of waking up to the delicious aroma of Parker House sausages sizzling in her favorite black frying pan. Along with the sausages, we would have golden-topped biscuits, piping hot and fresh out of the oven, hominy grits and scrambled eggs, washed down with a big glass of chilled orange juice.

Sometimes I would see Grandmother crying. I didn't understand the tears back then, but I understand them now. Grandmother carried a heavy burden. As a young girl, she had been taught the Word of God and the foundational principles of Holiness. However, as she grew up, she grew farther and farther away from God and began living a lifestyle that was contrary to all she had been taught. The choices she made put so much distance between her and

God until all she had left were her memories of sweet fellowship with the Lord in prayer and a few old gospel songs.

Throughout the week, Grandmother worked diligently around the house while Grandfather went to work. There was never a week – Monday through Friday – that Grandmother did not prepare a hot meal; however the weekends told quite a different tale. My siblings and I were left to fend for ourselves, with me in charge.

Friday through Sunday set the stage for Grandmother's alternate life. Grandmother partied and gambled all weekend, starting on Friday evening at Aunt Sarah's house. There she played Pity Pat, Tonk and Bid Whist while drinking Old Grand Dad and listening to dusty records. Some of her favorite tunes were *Put On Your Red Dress*, *Shot Gun* and *Stoop Down*. After warming up at Aunt Sarah's place, Grandmother would hit a few of her gambling spots on Lake Street, then end the night at the *Banner Lounge* on Walnut, where Grandfather would meet her after he got off work.

When I would return from school on Fridays, Grandmother would already be preparing for her "good time." Her girdle and stockings were always laid out neatly on her bed. She would always be standing in front of the dresser with the double-wide mirror, listening to her good time music and being extra careful not to mess up her good time make up she had already applied. Sometimes I propped myself up at the top of her bed and watched her in amusement as she struggled, grunted and moaned in a heated battle of tug-of-war with her girdle. It was Grandmother against the power of Lycra. It did not make a difference which girdle she chose, they all seemed to fight. The tussle was brutal, strenuous, breathtaking, and even offensive. The girdles tried to please her in a most commendable way by stretching themselves far beyond their capacity. But the girdles always ran into big problems: Grandmother's thighs. I truly believe that if those girdles could talk, the world would know they lived in fear of weekends and Grandmother's thighs.

After a long bout of heaving, Grandmother would finally ask me to snap the girdle onto her stockings. At first, I thought it was an honor, but after my first try, I learned otherwise. "Pull, pull! Com'on baby, do it for Grandma," she would say. I tried and tried, honestly, I tried. I tried to stuff all that fat into the leg of Grandmother's girdle, but my small hand would sink deeply into the roll of lard protruding from beneath the elastic band. Eventually, after poking, pulling and wiping several rounds of sweat from my brow, alas: girdle snapped to stockings. I would smile, feeling proud of my victory, but the victory always left me so exhausted that I had to take a nap. Those naps were some of my best sleep. I am eternally grateful for the invention of the nap!

On Saturday mornings Grandmother would call me from her bedroom, where she stayed all day hung-over from the night before. "Niecy...Niecy, come here, baby." Her request was for the same thing every time. "I need you to go to Mr. Nate's corner store and get Grandma a can of tomato juice and a pack of Stand Backs for my headache. Can you do that for Grandma, baby?"

I didn't mind because it gave me a chance to soak up some of the morning sun. I always enjoyed early morning walks. When I returned from the store, Grandmother would always let me keep the change. Although I knew that she was going to give it to me, I would hand it to her anyway, just so I could hear her say, "That's yours Niecy, for being Grandma's big girl." Then I would smile and skip away happy.

Because I was the eldest, I was in charge of keeping my brother and two sisters quiet. We sat around the house all weekend, eating cold cereal and toast that I made in the oven while watching cartoons, *Bewitched* and *Mr. Ed.*

Sometime late in the day, Grandmother would drag out of bed to prepare for her evening frolicking. She'd peep in on us, but only for a moment. "Y'all alright, Niecy? Did they eat?" I liked to see her smile when I told her that I had fed everyone. "That's my big girl," she would say.

One weekend, when I was five or six years old, Grandmother allowed my teenage uncle and his friend to babysit while she went out gambling. While we were playing Hide-and-Seek, my uncle coaxed me into hiding in a closet with him. I remember feeling the sleeves and hems of the clothes brushing against my face and trying not to giggle. As I stood against the mildewing closet wall, my uncle got on his knees and pulled me in front of him. He was breathing heavily as he pressed his heavy body against my small frame. I remember shifting my head from side to side, trying to keep him from kissing me. I was too young to understand what was happening, but I knew my uncle's body felt funny and I did not like what he was doing to me.

That was my uncle's first time violating me, but certainly not his last. His violation against me was the start of a cycle of incest that would plague me for many years. By the time I was seven years old, both male and female cousins would frequently kiss and grind on me, and Grandfather, whom I trusted and loved dearly, began taking advantage of me as well. Whenever he felt an incestuous urge, he would straddle me over his leg and bounce me up and down on his private part, while kissing me and sticking his tongue in my mouth. I would try turning my head to get away from his prickly beard and smelly alcohol-breath, but he always overpowered me.

Although I did not like any of their actions, it never occurred to me to talk to my mother about it. My mother had begun her own descent into street life; she had no time or interest in my needs or problems. Perhaps I could have told my grandmother, but that did not occur to me either. My existence grew more and more confusing as the incest continued. I felt like the chicken plate that we passed around at the dinner table, as if I wore a sign inviting everyone to take a piece of me. Feeling isolated and alone, I suffered in silence.

* * *

Having children did not slow my mother down. She relentlessly continued her negligence by hanging out with Little Rose, Carrie and Ulla Mae. These were her street friends, her "family," and they became her way of life. I wouldn't say they were solely responsible for her behavior, because Mother had a mind of her own, but they surely contributed to her demise.

Who Said It Couldn't Be Done?

Mother did not have a job and she didn't intend to get one; neither did she complete high school. Her ends were met through welfare and hustling. She gave Grandmother the food stamps to avoid hearing her complain about the awful job she was doing at taking care of us. However, Mother always fled with the cash, rushing back to her life of hustling, stealing, getting high, and hanging out at the pool hall. Although Mother wasn't around as much as we would have liked, there were times when she stayed around for a little while. During those times, she came bearing gifts: the wonderful treasures she had stolen or swindled out of others. There were a few weekends when she felt generous enough to take us to her apartment in the Washington Hotel. She had one of the nicest apartments in the building and while we were there, all we lacked was her love and affection. She would drop us off and leave us there alone the entire weekend, but at least we got to see her for the eight minutes it took to drive there from Grandmother's house.

*   *   *

Despite Mother's neglect, we had a good life; Grandmother made sure of that. She would always buy us the nicest clothes from the thrift store. My dresses and jumpers looked like they were new. I can still remember how Grandmother toiled; bent over the bathtub, sweat dripping from her brow, humming *Lord, Don't Move My Mountain.* Her melodious voice would echo out of the tiny bathroom and down the hallway, loud enough for me to hear her in my room. She would soak the jumpers in Argo starch and then run them up and down the washboard. The work would get so tedious that she would have a fan plugged in the bathroom, blowing across her back to cool her off. Sometimes I would stand in the doorway of the bathroom playing with my baby doll while watching Grandmother work and listening to her hum. Many times after she finished with the laundry, she would stay down on her knees a good while, singing and humming to herself. In her seasoned age, it was hard for her to lift herself up from the floor. I saw the way she struggled, grunting softly, pushing herself up on the side of the tub, trying to get up off her knees so that she could take the wet laundry outside in the back yard to be hung up on the clothesline to dry. But through all that grunting and struggling to pull herself up from the floor, whenever I was there, she always managed to squeeze out a smile just for me and say, "There's Grandma's baby." Ooooh, how I loved Grandmother!

One day, while Grandmother was outside hanging the laundry, I could hear her calling for me. "Niecy, where's Grandma's baby? Come on out here in this back yard." I laid my baby doll down on the bed and ran outside where Grandmother was. "You are getting big now," she said. "You can help your old Grandma." My first task was learning how to hang up clothes.

"Wait, now," Grandmother said laughing, while playfully snapping at my long, skinny legs with a clothespin. "You not stretching em' out enough. If you have too much sagging in the middle, they will take too long to dry. Here, do it like this." I loved working with Grandmother. She was so patient and caring that whatever she was willing to teach, I was willing to learn. I learned how to wash, dry and put away the dishes; mop the floor; and fold clothes, stacking them neatly in a pile without them falling. It amazed me that Grandmother was able to fold clothes so neatly and stack them almost as tall as a tree without them falling over. That was lots of fun! My favorite chore was cleaning the bathroom. I learned to remove rust from the sink, tub and toilet. I always loved it when she let me in on one of her housekeeping secrets. "Just take your time and do it right," she would say. I had fun learning how to do all my chores, except making the bed. It seemed to be the most tedious task out of them all, but I knew it had to be done. I can't remember if it was tedious because I had to do it everyday or because I felt forced to do it, I just know for sure I didn't like it.

"Niecy, Grandmother has a surprise for her baby," she called to me one day. "Go on in there and make your bed, and I'll give it to you when you are done." Oh, how I wanted what Grandmother had for me! I rushed through the bed-making exercise and I must say, it was the sloppiest bed I had ever made. I hoped Grandmother wouldn't notice, but when Grandmother came into the room to examine my work, she pulled everything off the bed; she even shook the pillows out of their cases. I was so afraid that I wouldn't get the gift Grandmother had for me that I wanted to cry. I did cry. "I want my gift," I wailed.

"Fix it how Grandma showed you and then you can get what I have for you. I know you can do it because you Grandma's big girl!"

My sister, Regina, was standing in the doorway teasing me. I wanted to yell at her for laughing, but I knew that it would only get me in more trouble. Although I was embarrassed, I continued in my effort to make the bed according to Grandmother's standards. After several hours of failed attempts to make hospital folds in the corners, I finally got it right and passed Grandmother's second examination with flying colors. It made me feel proud to know that I was back in her good graces, but it made me feel even better that she was still willing to give me the present she had for me. As she led me into the living room, I had butterflies in my stomach. I had been asking her for this pretty dress I saw in a store window downtown and she knew how much I wanted it, so maybe that was going to be it.

To my dismay, my surprise was a small ironing board and iron. It turned out that my next task was learning how to iron. Grandmother set up the ironing board in the living room, right in front of the television, so I wouldn't get bored with the monotony of all that ironing. By now, all of my chores were getting old. At first it was fun and exciting, but I soon realized that ironing and all of the other chores were nothing but work.

*   *   *

When I was in second grade, I started visiting my Aunt Mable and Uncle Ivan occasionally on the weekends. There wasn't much to do when I was over there, but being away from home provided me a way out of doing all of those chores. One particular weekend, the water was shut off in their building so it gave me an excuse to play in the water gushing from the fire hydrant down the street. Both old and young people alike were playing in the water, but I liked to drink it. The water tasted like it came straight from the faucet and I could have as much as I wanted. I had no idea it could make me sick. Shortly after drinking from the hydrant, I developed a terrible sore throat, felt weak and dizzy, and had difficulty breathing and swallowing. Aunt Mable thought I might be coming down with a cold or something, because all I did for the rest of my visit was lay around.

I was still feeling sick when I returned from school the following Monday. When I walked into Grandmother's house, I was surprised to find my mother and Grandmother sitting in the living room talking. It was good that my mother happened to drop in that day, because I became severely ill as the evening progressed and she ended up taking me to Rush Presbyterian Hospital, where I was diagnosed with diphtheria. Immediately they admitted me and began treating me with antibiotics. The doctor told my mother I could have died if she hadn't brought me to the hospital when she did.

My hospital stay lasted two months. I was relieved that it kept me from having to do chores but best of all, I didn't have to go to school. Although my family came to visit me regularly, I still got homesick and missed Grandmother's cooking. When I was released from the hospital, my family welcomed me home with warm, loving arms and a ton of presents. When I found out that Grandmother prepared a big bowl of strawberry Jell-O and a butter pound cake just for me, I didn't know whether to jump up and down or just start digging in. I was so glad to be back home!

Being out of school and getting out of doing chores was fun while it lasted, but it was now near the end of the school year and there wasn't enough time to catch up on all of the schoolwork I had missed. Administration told my grandparents that I would not be passing to the next grade with the rest of my classmates. This only compounded all of the other pressures I was dealing with: uncles and cousins molesting me; grandfather's beard, sour tongue and hot breath; and wondering why my mother didn't love me.

My self-esteem plummeted more and more. When I returned to school the following year, former classmates laughed at me and called me "dumb-dumb" and "stupid" because I had been held back. I did not want to be bullied and teased so I became very defensive. No longer was I eager to befriend others. I started closing myself off. I did not want to be with children younger than myself. I was already the tallest in my class, to be the oldest as well was overwhelming. Greatly discouraged, I remember thinking, *what's the use of going to school anyway?* From that point on, I lost all interest in school and made my mind up that I was going to drop out.

My aunt and uncle felt guilty that I had gotten sick under their supervision, so they tried to make up for it by spoiling me. I may not have been the smartest scholar in my peer's eyes, but I was definitely the best looking. Auntie Mable made sure I went to the beauty parlor every time I visited to get either a perm or a touch-up. All the stylists knew my favorite hairstyle: afro-puff pom-poms. Each time it was the same routine. The stylists would part my hair straight down the middle and put two ponytails high up on my head, lined up with my ears. They would apply a heavy pomade to slick down the baby hair around my face. The final touch was two gigantic afro-puffs; one propped on the left side of my head, the other on the right side. I walked away proud as a peacock. The stylists would tell me how cute I was and my grin would cover my entire face. Auntie Mable would get tickled pink and her smile would be just as wide as mine.

After leaving the salon, we always headed to the Plaza to shop for a new outfit. Auntie Mable would let me pick the outfit out myself, a privilege I did not have with Grandmother. I seized the moment and picked out whatever

I wanted. My favorite outfit was my yellow and white culottes with a cute white blouse and black fish net stockings. The outfit was not appropriate for a girl my age, but I liked looking older than I was. It helped ease the pain of being older than everyone else in my class. "Oooh, Niecy Bone don't look like a bone no more. Look at you, girl!" Aunt Mable said when I came out of the fitting room. Aunt Mable called me Niecy Bone because I was tall and slender, but that outfit brought out all of my curves.

Aunt Mable worked full time at a currency exchange, and Uncle Ivan owned neighborhood a liquor store. They always tried to get me the best of everything. I can remember on one of my visits, I saw some of the neighborhood children outside roller-skating. Sitting in the living room window, I cried like a beg baby because I didn't have any skates. Eventually I got up and walked around the corner to Uncle Ivan's store.

"What's wrong, TC (Topcat)?" Uncle Ivan said to me.

Sniff, sniff…"I want some skates," I said, with my eyes squeezed tightly shut. My nose started to drip because of all the waterworks, so I wiped it with my sleeve.

"Don't do that, TC; you're going to ruin your clothes like that," he said handing me his handkerchief.

"From the way you're crying, I thought someone beat you up or something. You mean that's all that's wrong? My TC is messing up that pretty little face over some roller skates? You mean I don't have to take my belt off to none of these little boys around here?"

"Naw," I said, still sniffling and whining. "I just want some roller skates."

"Well then, stop crying. We'll go get them tomorrow," he said, patting me on my back.

The next day Uncle Ivan purchased a pair of Precision roller skates. Precision skates were the top-of-the-line at the time and I was the toast of the neighborhood with those skates. I learned how to skate forward, backward, on one foot, holding on to the back of a bike, holding hands with my friends, uphill and downhill. I finally got so good I could skate and dance at the same time. I had so much fun! I was a skating phenomenon. I gave Uncle Ivan lots of hugs and kisses to thank him and he let me take my skates back to Grandmother's house with me. He was my favorite uncle. A few years later, he died and I miss him to this day.

*   *   *

One afternoon, I came home from school and my mother was at Grandmother's house. She and Grandmother were in the living room arguing because my mother wanted to take me and my brothers and sisters away from Grandmother. She had gotten a place to live and decided it was time that we lived with her.

"You cannot just prance up in here like this, without warning and just rip these children out of the only home they have known. I've been taking care of these children all these years, Annie. You haven't been here. What is wrong with you, girl? Huh? What is wrong with you? You are not stable, Annie. You are not ready to settle down. All you do is run the street and God knows what else. I'm not going to let you mess up these children like that. Now, go on back to where you came from and leave these children be, now, leave em' be! You hear me? Leave em be!"

"They mine," Mother protested, "they mine and I'm taking them with me. They belong to me and that's where they gonna be. Now, I'm not here to be fussing and fighting with you. All I want is what's mine. I'm gon get my children and a few of their things and be out of your house."

Grandmother seemed to give up fighting. She could see that my mother was at least putting forth a good effort by getting a place for us to stay. She desperately wanted to believe that her precious Annie Mae had finally changed and was going to do right by her children. Grandmother drew her apron to her hot, tear-stained face and wiped off the sweat and tears, then sank back into the sofa. "Tell me, Annie Mae, why you have to drag them way over to the other side of town? At least you could have gotten a place close by. And how are you going to take care of them? You don't have a job. You are not planning on doing anything illegal are you, Annie Mae?"

Mother did not answer. She rolled her eyes coldly and turned her back sharply to Grandmother. To her surprise, there I was staring her straight in the face. Our eyes locked, but I was unable to keep my eyes locked on hers for long. Her stare was piercing; it melted me the way rain melts the snow. I dropped my head and became a ball of emotions propped up on two wobbly legs. Slowly I lifted my head and admired how lovely my mother looked that day; what a beautiful woman she was. A thick group of freshly permed curls fell across her rosy cheek, softening her usual, non-emotional expression. The remaining locks rested on her thin neck and flowed past her bony shoulders, down to the middle of her sleek back. She was stunning. I loved her. But at nine years old, I was torn. I was faced with adapting to yet another situation. A part of me wanted to go with my mother, but I really did not know her. I wondered if all she said was going to be real this time. Would she really take us with her, or was this just another empty promise, another false hope? The insecure part of me feared the unknown and needed to cling to the security of what was certain. Grandmother was dependable and I trusted her.

All of my debating turned out to be unnecessary because my mother had already decided my fate. "Denise, go in the kitchen and get one of those big, green garbage bags and fill it up with some of y'alls clothes while I finish talking to your Grandma." I dropped my schoolbooks right there and hurried to do as she ordered. I rummaged through each of our drawers, grabbing piles of our neatly folded clothing and tossing it into the garbage bag. I filled one with clothes, and then ran back for another bag to hold some of our toys.

That day Mother hauled all five of us to the twelfth floor of Rockwell Gardens housing project, located on Van Buren and Campbell, on the west side of Chicago. The apartment was not much to look at, but we were going to have to get used to it because it was going to be home. It was a typical project apartment, with flat grayish-white walls and pale concrete floors, the kind of floors in a prison cell. The sour residue of urine resonated throughout the hallways of the building; it was always strong and always there. I hated walking up those stairs, but the elevator was no different; it reeked of urine as well.

The apartment did not feel like home the way Grandmother's house felt, but Mother was hustling hard to make money to fix things up and make us comfortable. Not long after we moved in, we came home from school one day and the entire apartment looked different. All of the walls had been freshly painted with the most brilliant colors I had ever seen: hues of reds and blues and warm marmalades were painted throughout the entire apartment, balanced with hints of beige, soft whites and tender pinks.

The curtains stood tall and statuesque at the windows; their commanding floral prints were drawn with elegant tiebacks and their lacey counterparts stretched in full beauty. Corresponding carpets lay in each bedroom to offset the freshly painted walls. There was new furniture in the living room, kitchen and each bedroom.

Mother wasn't there to see my face light up, but that was a special moment for me. I was so proud of her. I grinned as I ran from room to room saying, "Wow! Wow!" The thought of how Mother garnered all of the goods did not enter my mind. All I thought was *where is she? Where is our Mother? When will she return?* Nonetheless, things were finally coming together. The apartment was starting to feel like home. The nice things made my mother's absence a little more bearable. I remember feeling as if I could be happy there.

6

HOME ALONE

A couple of years passed and so did the thought of happiness. Mother was never around, nor were any of our fathers. Mother stopped in the projects for a few minutes once or twice a week, and on welfare check day to drop off a few food stamps but otherwise, she was gone. I tried to let my mother know how I felt about her absence and that I didn't approve of her lifestyle, but all I received were looks of contempt and blows to the face, hard enough to land me on the floor. I was not allowed to express my feelings about her absence; Mother considered that disrespectfully talking back and trying to control her. All I was trying to do was let her know that I loved her and loved living with her, but I missed her when she didn't come home. I also wanted to know why she took us from Grandmother's house if she did not want to stick around and care for us. However, my mother wasn't about to explain herself to me. I was her child; she didn't answer to me and that was that. She made sure I knew I was not going to control her, which was demonstrated the very first time I tried expressing my feelings. All I remember is picking myself up off the floor. Her hands were quick, almost invisible. I was definitely not up to the challenge. So I learned to just take the food stamps, shut my mouth and quietly watch her drive away.

At the local *Hi-Low Food Store*, I tried stretching the food stamps into enough food to feed five, sometimes six people. Often we hungrily waited for her to stop by again with another small ration. At times, I was so hungry and angry that I felt totally destructive. I wanted to tear things up; I wanted to hit and break things. I wanted to bite and scratch, and savagely gnaw. I wanted the pain to go away. I wanted my mother.

We started out in the projects as somewhat of a family, acquiring all the things we needed: food, toys, furniture, name-brand clothing, education, and – for a short while – a mother. As time progressed, I stopped going to school regularly because the responsibility of caring for my younger brothers and sisters was too much for me. I was overwhelmed with having to serve as both father and mother to them in spite of being a child myself. Yet I was determined to provide for and protect the little ones. Every night I made sure the door was locked and everyone was accounted for. I protected them from bullies in the neighborhood and disciplined them when necessary. I prepared breakfast for everyone. Their favorite meal was scrambled eggs, bacon, toast and sometimes cold cereal, if we had any. After a good breakfast, I would make sure that they were off to school on time. When the food stamps ran out – and they always did – I would figure out a way to feed my family, and I didn't care if it meant that I had to beg or steal in order to make sure we ate. Many days I would send the little ones out to borrow needed food items from neighbors in our building. One would borrow bread, the other eggs, and a third would borrow butter. This process continued until I scrounged up enough items to prepare a tasty meal. Sometimes this method of collection was unsuccessful and many days we had only sugar or syrup water to drink, and mayonnaise or mustard sandwiches to eat.

One day when I couldn't scrounge up one crumb from anywhere, I called Grandmother to tell her we didn't have any food. In no time, Grandfather brought us some groceries and Grandmother was right there on the phone, giving me instructions on how to prepare the various foods. She told me how to snap the green beans and discard their thin tips, how to wash the pigtails and neck bones, then boil them in a big pot with just the right amount of water and special seasonings. Lastly, she taught me how to make her delicious recipe for homemade cornbread. Everything turned out perfectly. We were so grateful that Grandmother and Grandfather had saved the day – bon apétite!

At that point, we had not seen or heard from our mother in weeks, but life can be funny sometimes. Mother arrived home for one of her infrequent visits the very day Grandfather brought the groceries. Grandmother had asked me to call her whenever my mother showed up, so I went and called her and gave my mother the phone. Soon I heard them arguing and Mother was getting louder and louder. Grandmother was threatening to call DCFS if my mother didn't stop neglecting us. "Do what you want to do," I heard my mother say. "These are my kids and I take care of them. You don't know what's going on over here because you don't live here. We got food up in this house, and I ain't been gone nowhere. Just because I wasn't here when Daddy dropped that bag of groceries off don't mean nothing; I had something to do. I don't have to be up in this apartment twenty-four hours a day. I didn't ask y'all for nothing, we got food. You know how Denise likes to lie. Stop getting up in my business because you always think the worst of me anyway. These kids got everything they need. Stop trying to turn them against me because you want them back. How you going to sit up there and call the people on me and tell them to come and take my children?

Go ahead, call who you want to call!" my mother yelled, as she slammed the phone down in Grandmother's ear.

When Mother got off the phone, she yanked the cord out of the phone and right out of the wall. She grabbed me and began to threaten me. I was afraid. I could feel and smell her hot breath stinging the side of my face as she sneered in that familiar tone, "Who do you think you telling on, little girl? Huh? Do you think you big enough to tell on me? You think Momma gonna come over here and beat me? I'm grown. Didn't I tell you not to be calling nowhere unless I tell you to?"

Mother began slowly wrapping the phone cord around her hand to get a better grip, then she pushed me away and the beating commenced. "You think I'm scared of your Grandma? Huh? Is that what you think? You think telling on me is going to make me stay at home? What is your Grandmother going to do? Call the man? Well, let her call the man. Don't nobody want y'all but me. I'm your Momma, Denise. You hear me girl? *I'm* your Momma! *I* got this here roof over your head. *I* got them clothes on your back. *I* put food up in this house. Me! *I* do everything for y'all! Why you think I'm out hustling every day? For y'all, Denise, that's why. I'm doing my job, do you hear me? I'm a good mother. You hear me? I'm a good mother!"

Blistering welts popped up all over my body. With every threat and accusation came another whack across my legs, arms, chest and back. I fought hard to get away, but I was no match for Mother's rage. All I could do was bleed and beg. I begged Mother to stop beating me, but she seemed numb. "I will kill you if you ever call my mother again, do you hear me? Your grandmother don't run this up in here. Do you hear me, little girl? This here is my house, *my* house! I run this. You do what *I* say. All your orders come from me. If you don't get it from me, you don't act on it. Don't bring this kind of trouble up in my house no more. I mean I will kill you, bringing this mess up in here! Now get out of my face! Go get some alcohol and clean yourself up. Stanley, bring me a glass of water."

Mother's rage had passed and I had survived. Swiftly I hurried to get out of her path and hobbled my way to the bathroom. I could hear her voice in the background telling Stanley to find something to get the blood off the floor. Pricked like a pomegranate, I stood gazing in the mirror, broken hearted and broken spirited. I didn't understand why things were the way they were. As I dabbed my wounds with sorrowful tears in my eyes, I asked why. *Why, Mother?* I thought. *Why? Why you gotta be like that? Why you gotta be so mean? I can't stand you. You make me sick! What did we do to you that you have to treat us this way? Grandmother was good to us. She loved us. Why can't you be good to us? If all that stuff you told Grandmother is true, why don't you act like it? If you didn't want us, you should have left us there with her.* My heart was getting heavier by the minute. *Oh God*, I cried silently. *Why is she our Mother? Why don't she love us? Why we don't have no food? Why don't we have no clothes? Why don't we have no mother, God? Why don't we have no mother? What's wrong with us? What's wrong with us, God? Why you don't like us? What did we ever do?*

I could no longer see my reflection in the mirror because my vision was blurred from all of my tears. I took the bottle of alcohol and began to pour it over my wounds. I didn't mind the sting; I just let it burn. I remained in the bathroom for several hours nursing my broken heart.

Mother hung around the house for a few days after that incident. The next day she took me and Stanley hustling with her, to teach us the trade. She drove us through her stomping grounds. First, she took us to the senior citizen parking lot and showed us how to steal hubcaps by prying them off of parked cars with a screwdriver. Early the next morning, we took the hubcaps to the Maxwell Street market and sold them.

Our next few stops were Mother's dope spots on 16th and Central Park, and Red John's spot on Kedzie and Ogden. Lastly, she took us to the shooting gallery on 16th and Homan, but she wouldn't let us go in with her. As she was getting out of the car, she gave us our instructions. "Y'all sit tight and don't move. I'll be right back." We must have sat in that car for hours.

*   *   *

Mother had long since stopped bringing home the nice, name-brand clothes that I had grown to love. Having grown out of most of our nicer outfits, we were each left with only a few things to wear, so I had to wash our clothes quite often. The laundromat was only a few blocks from our apartment, so I tried to make it there whenever I could. Most of the time I did not have enough change for a single load, but I dared not call Grandmother to let her know. Often my siblings had to go to school in dirty clothes that were too small for them. Trying to be the head of a family at ten, eleven and twelve years old was overwhelming, but I was doing the best I could do.

Despite the chores and all of the other adult responsibilities that had been dumped on me, I did manage to have some time to play and get to know some of the other people in our building. Peaches was my closest friend. She lived at the far end of the "ramp" and had a brother named Mark, who was Stanley's best friend. Since we were all such good friends, people· in the building thought we would begin liking each other. I was expected to fall for Mark and Peaches was expected to fall for Stanley. Well, they were right; our hormones started running wild and we did start liking each other, but not as people predicted. My eyes fell on Peaches. My sexual attraction toward women was beginning to manifest. When the four of us played house together, I made sure that we put a new spin on the old game. Instead of the boys and girls becoming a family together, Peaches and I hooked up. And the boys…well, I really didn't care; they were free to play whatever they wanted: cap guns, marbles, it didn't matter to me. I had *my* family.

I also had three other close friends who lived next door to us and were sisters: Patti, Rossi and Loretta. Together we played Stand Back, where we took turns throwing a ball as far as we could away from one another. We also played Red Light, Green Light and Mr. Freeze. Although we were friends, the sisters were not always nice to me. Sometimes they liked hurting my feelings and making fun of me. My sister, Regina, had long, jet-black, wavy hair, which everyone admired. On the other hand, my hair was short, kinky and broken off in several spots. It was not manageable at all. No matter how much I brushed or combed it, or tried to lay it down with some grease, it would do its own thing. The three sisters regularly teased me by calling me "baldly locks," or by drawing a picture of an ugly girl with only a few squiggly strands of hair sticking up on the top of her head. Then they would point it towards my door and sing a mean chorus of Baldy Locks in my honor.

Another one of our next-door neighbors was a woman named Ruthie Jordan. When I first met her, she was an alcoholic and often threw wild parties on the weekends. Eventually she got saved and began attending *True Holiness Deliverance Ministry*, a small storefront sanctified church located on the south side of Chicago. Sometimes when we would be playing in the hall or running up and down the ramp, she would call us over and start telling us about Jesus. At that time, I didn't want to hear anything about Jesus, so I would laugh and mock her. Often she would sit out in the hallway with her children and read the Word of God. Sometimes I would overhear her and her children praying and praising God through the walls. The sound was so rhythmic and harmonious that I would put a cup against the wall so I could hear better. Those joyful praises were not like anything I ever heard.

I also spent time at Ulysses S. Grant Social Center, located near the projects. This was a community center where lots of the neighborhood children hung out after school and during the summer. The center sponsored a variety of after-school activities such as ping-pong, basketball, roller-skating and reading programs. I enjoyed roller-skating and ping-pong at the center, but I never found much use for their reading programs.

As my mother's dependence on narcotics and alcohol escalated, so did the neglect and abuse. She was away from home so much we had grown accustomed to her absence and hoped that she would stay away. We did not see her through the week very often, and she was always running the streets on Fridays and Saturdays, often returning on Sunday mornings just around daybreak. Mother wasn't a churchgoer, but some remote part of what Grandmother taught her about The Church of God In Christ organization must have stuck with her. Whenever she was at the apartment on a Sunday morning, she would turn the dial on the living room radio to a church station and listen to praise music, while she moseyed around the house, smoking her cigarettes.

God was foreign to my siblings and me; no one ever took us to church. The only talk I can recall about God in our home are times when Grandmother would sing those old church songs or talk about when she was a little girl growing up in the old Church of God in Christ. Sometimes she would reminisce about how she didn't wear pants, make-up or jewelry back in those days. She would also talk about how God used Evangelist Mattie B. Poole to raise my mother up from her sickbed when she was hit by a car and almost died. Despite our lack of spiritual upbringing, we developed our own form of worship. Often we "played church," and I always was the preacher. I would wrap myself in a white sheet, which represented a ministerial robe. My brother, Stanley played his beat-up drum set for our services, while my sisters, Regina and Benesse, acted as the church choir. I suppose that spoiled toddler Linzie was our congregation, because he wandered all around us as we preached and sang praise songs to God. I believe our gift of praise was a sweet-smelling sacrifice before God the King, and His Son Jesus Christ.

We did have a few old gospel records we sometimes played during our services on an old toy record player. The records sound scratchy, but we didn't mind. My favorite songs were *Sweet Home* and *Lord, Don't Move My Mountain*. I was especially fond of *Lord, Don't Move My Mountain* because the singer asked God for strength to conquer mountains of pain and trouble in her life, and not to just make them all go away. Even at that young age, the thought that God could give you strength to overcome obstacles in your life meant something to me. Already faced with so many challenges, I suppose I knew I was facing an uphill battle.

*   *   *

Often when I thought about the condition of my life, bitter hostility brewed inside me. I could feel anger and rage building around my disappointment. I resented having my childhood snatched away by all the tiresome adult responsibilities dumped on me in my mother's absence. I wanted to have nice, clean clothes that my mother washed and ironed for me. I wanted to hear her voice sweetly calling through the living room window, "Denise, it's time for supper; come on in and eat." I longed to feel her stroke my cheek, then kiss me gently and tell me she loved me. I wanted a dollhouse with lots of dolls. I wanted to go outside and run, jump, skip and play. I wanted my mother to hold me in her strong, secure arms when I was scared, and when I cried, I longed to have her wipe the tears from my eyes. When I had a problem, I wanted my mother to solve it. Late in the wee hours of the night, I wanted to feel a soft, cuddly blanket being gently pulled over my feet and shoulders, and a fluffy pillow tucked under my head. My mother was never there to do any of those things. Instead, I did my own laundry, my own cooking and my own cleaning. I wiped my own tears and reached down alongside the milk crates I slept on and grabbed my own sheet and spread it back over my cold feet, hoping to ease the biting chill I felt in my body; but mostly trying to warm the cold I felt in my heart. I cleaned the house, bathed my younger siblings, combed their hair and ironed their school clothes. I learned how to solve my own problems and figure out things by myself. I learned how to lie, how to cheat and how to steal. I learned how to connive and be tough, unfeeling and cold. I learned how to be just like my mother.

Over time, all of the nice furniture my mother bought when we first moved in to the projects wore out. One day my siblings and I came across a mattress someone had abandoned beside the dumpsters outside of our building, which we brought upstairs and placed on top of the milk crates. To anyone else it was garbage, but to us it was one of our most cherished pieces of furniture. Some of the cotton stuffing had come out, exposing the springs and wires, but it was still comfortable enough for the children to lie on and sleep peacefully. We also used the milk crates for chairs once our couches gave out, but were unable to scrounge up blankets or pillows to cushion them. When the children came home from school, we'd huddle around our slowly dying television to watch our favorite shows. We'd have to reposition the aluminum foil on the antenna several times in order to get a clear picture. When the television finally went out completely, we had nothing to do but wander aimlessly around the complex. My sad existence had become dark and obscure. I wasn't having fun. I wanted to die.

7

INTRODUCTIONS

"Y'all come on. You know I don't have time for all this slow poking around. When it's time to be there, it's time to be there." Mother had registered us for a two-week trip to North Dakota, sponsored by Mallic House, a Catholic Charities social service organization located near the projects. She learned of the program through a friend and decided it would get rid of us for a few weeks. She was rushing us because she didn't want us to miss our ride. Earlier I heard her on the phone talking to some of her friends about how she had big plans for the next couple of weeks, because she wouldn't have any distractions. She wanted to know if they were game for what she had in mind.

On the day we returned from our trip, Mother was supposed to meet us at the train station. We ended up waiting by the tracks for hours, sitting on our luggage and praying that we hadn't been forgotten. It was hard keeping hope alive once we began to see the sun set, and as the last bit of orange disappeared from the evening sky, I truly feared that we would be there all night. Mother finally arrived, but she wasn't the same.

Who Said It Couldn't Be Done?

Though darkness had fallen, I still could see Mother as she walked toward us. I had never seen her walk that way before. Her stride was smooth and had an easy, laid-back sleekness to it. I liked it. As she got closer, I noticed she was wearing all male attire. I checked out her rugged Levi's jeans with the matching vest, and her cowboy boots with the spurs. Her crisp, white button-down shirt pulled the whole outfit together. She looked like the last man. Her beautiful, silky curls were gone. She had replaced them with a radical – though well-groomed – reddish-blonde afro, topped with a genuine suede cowboy hat she tilted to the side. A small, red fire glowed from the cigarette she had smashed between her lips. There was a woman snuggled under her arm, giggling like a schoolgirl, and her running buddies, Candy and Spice were following closely behind.

It was in this abrupt way we learned our mother was bisexual and butch. Mother and I stood there, face to face, in another awkward moment where neither of us knew what to say. With the cigarette still dangling from the corner of her mouth, she looked each of us over and then in a flat, monotone drawl, ordered us to the car. As I turned to leave with the others, my mother grabbed my arm and held me back. "Candy and Spice, y'all go ahead with the small ones for me, and make sure they get in the car while I take care of this right quick. Hey, put them suitcases in the trunk for me – and don't slam my trunk either!"

When Candy and Spice got a reasonable distance away, Mother looked at her lady friend and introduced me. "This is Denise, my oldest." The woman looked at me politely, but did not speak. She was shorter than Mother with dark-brown skin, appeared to be pigeon-toed and seemed to have a warm personality. Mother looked back at me. "This here is Cathy. She's gonna be staying with us for a while." I didn't speak. "Now let's go," she said sharply.

I curled my lips tightly to stop the words from flying out of my mouth. I could feel them rolling off the tip of my tongue and pressing hard against my teeth. I could feel them trying to escape, like a round of bullets blasting from a gun. *Why are you always doing this to us? What is wrong with you? Why can't you do right? Why you look like that? Why you cut your hair? Why you dressed like a man? You ain't no man; you our momma. Why you got to be our momma? Why you late? Is she why you late? You been fooling round with your friend? Why you always got somebody with you? Oooh, I can't stand you! You make me sick. We've been sitting out here all day. We ain't ate or nothing and look at you, acting like you don't even care, like you ain't wrong. You know you wrong. Oooh, I can't*

81

stand you! I wanted to lay all of that on her in one fast-paced, non-stop round of shoot-em-up dialogue. Instead, I bit my lip until blood ran out of the side of my mouth.

The ride home was interesting. Mother's long Cadillac was stuffed to capacity: four adults, loud music, loud talking, loud perfume and five tired, hungry and confused children, wondering what happened to their mother. When we entered our apartment, there were more surprises: strange people, lots of them, everywhere. In the two weeks we were in North Dakota, my mother had turned our apartment completely out. It had become the new hangout for her freaky group of friends. Everywhere I looked, people were shooting dope, smoking marijuana, buying and selling drugs, getting drunk and throwing up all over the floors.

From that day on, our apartment was never the way we remembered it. Wild orgies took place on the weekends and there were usually gay couples in every room except ours during the week. Prostitutes would come by, hoping to make a little money or get high before hitting the stroll. Music blared day and night while card parties and crap games went on in the kitchen. And there, right in the middle of it all, was our mother. Mother had restricted us children to one room and told all of the freaks we were off limits. No one dared violate her command. Mother had a reputation for being treacherous, and no one had the courage to cross her.

One Saturday night, not long after we returned from North Dakota, I witnessed something that would affect me for the rest of my life. The apartment was full of men and women who had gathered for an initiation ceremony. In order to belong to the exclusive group of men and women who frequently held orgies at our apartment, you had to be formally initiated. This meant that the new member had to have sex with several of the other club members. On this particular night, there was a girl there by the name of Florence who was a virgin, and it was her initiation ceremony. I wanted to see what all the noise was that was coming from the living room, so I snuck out of our room, eased down the hall and leaned up against the wall by the living room, where I had a good view of all that was taking place. I was shocked to see this big, grown man named Tye on top of skinny, little Florence. Florence's head was turned to the side and tears were streaming down her face, but that did not seem to matter to Tye. Florence's body looked like it was convulsing in agony with each of Tye's powerful thrusts. I could see drops of blood on the floor beneath Florence's body. Although I didn't understand everything I was seeing, I knew one thing: Florence was not enjoying herself at all. Somewhat stunned, I slipped around the corner to where my mother was standing and asked her what was wrong and why Florence was crying like that. Without even realizing she was speaking to me, and without taking her eyes off of the main attraction, Mother answered coldly, "Ain't nothing wrong, she's just getting her virginity taken, that's all."

At that moment, I made up in my young mind that I would never have anything to do with men because they hurt women. In them, I saw no tenderness, no passion, care or concern; all I saw was doggish, brutal violation, and I wanted no part of it.

Mother had definitely changed. She was never warm or loving, but just when I thought she couldn't get any colder, she turned the thermostat down to the bottom of the dial and became a pimp. She had a string of women she pimped on a daily basis. I saw her pistol-whip them, take their money, tell them she loved them, then put them back out on the corner. Although she was only five feet six inches tall, with a medium build, she was cold clean through; everybody knew not to mess with her. Her street name was Dirty Old Man, but everyone called her Dirty O for short. As she continued to get deeper into the street life, the less we saw of our mother until Mother completely disappeared and all that was left was Dirty O.

Aside from all of the freaks, Cathy possessed a motherly sweetness and beautiful smile that made it easy for us to accept her. She became our new mom. She took us on outings and even intervened when Dirty O wanted to beat us for no apparent reason. If Dirty O had money left over after purchasing their dope, Cathy would go to *Groceryland* and buy us food. Most of the time all she was able to get was two cans of chili, a box of crackers and one 20-ounce bottle of pop, which she'd split between all of us, including herself and Dirty O. But for all of Cathy's kindness, it was her relationship with Dirty O that first initiated me into the gay life.

One of my morning chores was to prepare breakfast for Dirty O and Cathy, which I served to them on a tray in their bedroom. Often when I entered the room, I would notice a peculiar thing. Cathy would be sitting up with her back against the headboard, and Dirty O would be squirming around under the blanket, near the lower part of Cathy's body. When I would return some time later to remove the tray, their positions would be reversed. This ritual was intriguing; it tickled my curiosity. I mentioned it to Stanley one day, but he called me nosy and refused to talk about it. (Some years later, I learned Stanley had been just as nosy as I was.)

Cathy was mainly a social drinker, but there were times when she would get sloppy drunk. Dirty O had found a loving companion in Cathy, but that wasn't enough to slow her down and keep her off of the streets. She was on the run all of the time, pimping and hustling to make money for drugs, and Cathy was alone with us at home more frequently. Her role became more of a live-in babysitter than Dirty O's live-in lover and Cathy did not like that, so she took to the bottle from time to time.

One night Dirty O and Cathy got into a heated argument and it didn't end up very well. Even though the argument took place over the telephone, I could only imagine the insults and profane language Dirty O hurled at Cathy. Afterward, Cathy's hopelessness took a nose-dive and she drank herself into a stupor. This time she drank so much it seemed she had drank herself blind. Cathy locked herself in their bedroom and began destroying everything in sight. We couldn't see what she was doing, but the sound of shattering glass and loud thumps against the wall painted a crystal clear picture. After an hour or so, things quieted down; Cathy's sobbing ceased and the walls fell silent. Curious and a little worried, I went into the bedroom to check on Cathy. She wasn't my real mother, but I didn't want to lose the closest thing I had to one.

When I went into the room, Cathy was lying across the bed. Gently I nudged her arm and called out her name, but she did not respond. I tried again, but still no response. I nudged her a few more times and still nothing. Then I began to notice her petite, curvy, brown frame. All she had on was a lace bra and a small pair of matching lace underwear. Thoughts began racing through my mind and suddenly I didn't want her to wake up. I nudged her again, except this time I gently nudged her breast. It was soft and I liked how it felt. I nudged it again. I leaned forward and placed my face on her neck so that I could smell her body. She moaned a little at my advances. Apprehensively, I moved my face from her neck until my nose brushed the nipple of her breast. She made more groaning noises so I explored further. I didn't know much about sex, aside from what I had witnessed by watching the freaks in our apartment, but I certainly wanted to learn. Slowly, I slid my hand in her underwear and began fondling her. Her moans became louder and frightened me. "Cathy, Cathy, are you okay?" I asked nervously, pulling my hand out of her panties and hoping that I hadn't awakened her with my inquisitiveness. To my surprise, she remained silent and signaled that she was ready for more by turning completely onto her back and spreading her legs slightly.

That was my first willful sexual encounter and I must say, I was hooked. From that point on, I saw females in a very different light. The more Dirty O stayed away from the house, the drunker Cathy would get, and I looked forward to comforting her.

*   *   *

Household chores and responsibilities began to increase as my siblings got older and I couldn't keep up with all of the work by myself. Nor did I want to. It got to be so overwhelming that I reached a point where I didn't want to do anything at all. If my siblings and Cathy weren't willing to lend a hand, I didn't feel like I should carry the entire load alone.

I had stopped going to school on a regular basis a few years earlier, and finally I stopped going at all. Stanley followed my lead shortly after. Truant officers and school officials had given up trying to locate us – or our mother – so we just stayed at home. He and I did the best we could to keep our younger siblings' clean and neat so they could go to school without being embarrassed about their appearance, like Stanley and I had been. We would wash their clothes in the bathtub, and since we didn't have clothespins or a clothesline, we hung them up to dry on the cabinet doors above the stove. Sometimes the clothes caught on fire, but we were always able to stomp out the flames before any real damage was done. The younger children didn't complain, but it wouldn't have mattered if they did, because they had no choice but to wear what we provided.

When we could scrounge up enough change, we would take all the clothes to the laundromat down the block. One time, a couple of our neighbors were there while Stanley and I were doing our laundry. One of them noticed all of the men's clothes – the silky boxer shorts with matching tee shirts and the Fruit of the Loom briefs – and started asking us whose clothes those were. "Whose draws are those? I thought you didn't have no daddy. Where's your momma's clothes?" Not knowing what to say, and being too ashamed to say that those were our momma's clothes, neither Stanley nor I said anything; we just kept folding the clothes and stuffing them in a garbage bag.

When it finally got to the point where I couldn't take all the pressure anymore, I ran away to my Grandmother's house where things were warm and clean; the only place where I remembered feeling loved.

Grandmother did her best to fix all the damage my mother had done. She wanted me to be a child again, but all I had experienced had changed me.

Grandmother enrolled me in Corky Elementary School and you can believe that being back in school took some getting used to. I hadn't been to school consistently since fourth grade. With only two weeks left in the school year, the administrators placed me in eighth grade because of my age. My academic achievements and learning capabilities were far from that of the average eighth grader, but I was happy to participate in the graduation ceremony in spite of my academic deficiencies. Besides, I was preparing to receive an education of another sort: Streetology.

8

INITIATIONS

Dirty O put a milk crate on the floor in the middle of the room, upon which she laid a large piece of wood. This became her workstation. On the workstation, she placed some of the items that were to be used: a spoon, cigarette lighter, a wine bottle cap with a bobby pin attached, a syringe (sometimes five syringes or more), bags of dope (lots of bags of dope, spread out) and cotton bitten from cigarette filters by teeth that were always hungry. Sitting side-by-side were two jars filled with water: one contained clear water and the other murky water. There were folding chairs in the room; five maybe six, sometimes seven folding chairs. She would always find another folding chair and drag it into that room. Never the living room, never the kitchen; it was always dragged to *that* room. That room always craved another chair. Some of the chairs were old and damaged and the paint was scratched down to the steel. Blood was on the chairs. Frantically the junkies sat upon those folding chairs, with fidgeting fingers; tapping, pounding, scratching…and scratching harder. The light was always on in that room and I saw the junkies. The room had a yellow cast, but I still saw them. I saw Dirty O in the room. I saw unfamiliar faces become familiar faces in the room. I saw them sitting, leaning, slouching, nodding on folding chairs; I saw them beating their arm – whipping it, rubbing it, pinching it – searching for a passage inside, where it was dark and lonely and nothing was moving at all.

Death was in the room. Death was always in the room, lurking treacherously and staring hard at the folding chairs. His dark eyes were set on the folding chairs. Death saw Candy with the needle stuck in her arm and he became very quiet. Death was choking her. I could hear the gurgling sounds in her throat and I could see the foam running out of her mouth. When she didn't move, I didn't move. I cried soundless tears. I couldn't see her chest racing up and down anymore. Slow, slower, slow again…then nothing. She stopped breathing; she stopped gurgling. Her head swung back and hit the wall behind her. Her pupils disappeared as her eyes rolled into the back of her head, then she slumped over and with one big thump, Candy hit the floor.

Dirty O cursed, pulled her syringe out of the glass filled with clear water, then pushed away from the slab of wood. The room was filled with the gray haze of cigarette smoke. Standing over the unmoving body, the cigarette still dangling from her mouth, she spoke. "Denise, go get Stanley."

Stanley dragged the wilted body into the bathroom then lifted it into the tub and covered it with cold water. When Candy resuscitated minutes later, she went right back into the room and sat upon a folding chair. My little sisters screamed hysterically as they saw a swamp monster trudging through their house, crying and scratching and looking for a folding chair. I was afraid. I didn't want to go back into that room, but I was powerless to its pull. It knew me. It knew my name. The room was calling me by my name. I was chosen to sit upon a folding chair. It called me in a hypnotic baritone; I had to go. I was destined to go in the room and sit upon a folding chair.

*   *   *

I could feel myself changing inside. My emotions, my desires, my cravings: they all turned dark. They were insatiable; I was insatiably addicted to living life fast. I craved the low-end excitement and drama that was a part of Dirty O's lifestyle. I yearned for it; I needed it. The part of me that longed for the Brady Bunch lifestyle no longer existed. Darkness emerged from a long sleep and took control of my life.

Who Said It Couldn't Be Done?

I began to steal $100 bills from inside Grandmother's lampshade to give Dirty O as a way of bribing her to let me hang with her at her dope spots and in the taverns along Pulaski and Fifth Avenue. Grandmother never missed the money; it was part of a settlement from her former husband's estate. Because of my lack of education, I did not know the different monetary denominations, so I believed Dirty O when she said I had taken $10 bills instead of $100 bills. She would say we'd split the money fifty-fifty, then give me five dollars back. Eventually I learned the difference and got all riled up when I realized Dirty O had been cheating me. The irony is that I had been cheating Grandmother by stealing the money from her in the first place! I guess my desire to be with Dirty O, and experience the excitement she found in the streets, overpowered any sense of loyalty or understanding of right and wrong.

At one of Dirty O's favorite taverns, I met a prostitute named Renee, who had a female pimp named Don. Renee looked real good to me. She wore a red, curly wig and thigh-high boots. One night I told the bartender to send her a drink on me, which I paid for with money I had stolen from Grandmother. Every time I went to the tavern, Renee was there and I would tease her as if I wanted to get with her. One day she collared me and told me I was either going to be all the way "in the game" or I better "stop teasing her." I had never been in that situation before, so feeling a little intimidated, I left her alone.

It was inevitable that I would begin my own experimentation with drugs. After all, I had observed my mother and her friends shooting up and appearing to enjoy themselves for years. It seemed that the next logical step was for me to share the bliss with them. Therefore, when the day finally came when Dirty O sent me *by myself* to pick up her dope package from Red John's on Kedzie and Ogden, I stole two bags of heroin out of the package. When Dirty O finished shooting the drugs and left out of the apartment, I went directly to the bathroom to retrieve her work kit. I pounded against the radiator and the kit popped out, falling to the floor in front of me. I ran bath water to create a good reason for being in the bathroom for such a long time. Next I cooked the dope the way I watched Dirty O do so many times. I extracted the cotton from a cigarette filter and placed it into a spoon to draw up the dope. I tied my wrist with a stocking until my veins stood up. In my right hand, I held the syringe and took my time plunging it into my vein. I wanted to feel what Dirty O felt when she shot dope. Slowly I pushed the drugs in, but since I was new at heroin use, I forgot to un-tie the stocking from my wrist. Blood and heroin mingled in my vein and swiftly flowed through the tied part of my arm. When a huge knot rose up on my hand, I quickly untied the stocking and everything in the knot rushed to my head. I immediately began vomiting explosively as my body tried to reject the drugs. I thought I was dying.

Still vomiting, I stumbled out of the bathroom. In a wild frenzy, I made my way to the next building, where a group of experienced drug users was shooting up. They calmed me down and assured me that I was not dying, I was just inexperienced. An older woman instructed me to relax and wait for the rush to set in. I listened to what she said and she was right; immediately I began to nod. Warm, good feelings began flowing through me and a delightful sensation of peace and comfort came over me. I remember thinking that was what I'd been looking for. Years of anger and hatred, fear and disappointment, abuse and neglect, molestation and betrayal seemingly evaporated from my consciousness. The fear of Grandfather's lap and dark closets; male cousins and Dirty O's friends; the pain of lonely nights and crying for my mommy; being hungry and scared; punching walls and throwing things all slowly and rhythmically dripped out of my twelve year old body. Soft tears flowed from my eyes. I took a deep breath in and then exhaled. *Aaaah! I like this. I feel sooo good.* My stress and worries melted away and all I wanted to do was nod and sleep my peaceful sleep. The world around me turned, but for once in my life I was still. *This is it! This is what I've been looking for. Mmm, I love dope.*

Suddenly, seemingly out of nowhere I was approached by Renee, the prostitute I knew from the tavern on Pulaski. I had no idea she knew some of the same people I knew. Forcefully, she grabbed my arm and led me into the washroom, where she reminded me of the ultimatum she had previously given me. I could hear in her voice that she was not playing and I was afraid. She told me to get out of my clothes and lie down on the floor. I refused, but she repeated herself, more emphatically. When I refused again, she reached down in her breast area, pulled out a straightedge razor and began cutting my clothes off. When she told me again to lie on the floor, I followed her command without saying another word. She then proceeded to perform oral sex on me.

When she was finished, she told me I could go and warned me to watch who I played around with. I got up quickly, grabbed my clothes and hurried out of the apartment. Outside of the building I saw a police officer and told him I wanted to press charges for rape, but the officer did not believe my story. They had never heard of a female raping another female, so I had to let it go. After that incident, I would see Renee from time to time, but never had anything to do with her. Sometime later, I heard a trick had raped and killed her.

*   *   *

I became Dirty O's new road-dog, and I continued shooting dope without her knowledge. My siblings were left in the care of whatever woman Dirty O had living with her at the time and she and I hit the streets. Dirty O taught Stanley and me how to pop hubcaps off cars and sell them on Maxwell Street. The money went for her drug habit, but she would give each of us a few dollars for helping her out. I would take my money and hook up with Bernice and Smokey, two of Dirty O's friends, who both sold and used drugs. I had been shooting dope with them almost a year and Dirty O never found out.

One hot summer day, Dirty O came to Bernice's house to get high and I was there, sitting on the tub in the bathroom with a needle dangling from my arm. Dirty O was so angry that she pulled her pistol out and was ready to kill Bernice, accusing her of selling me drugs and getting me high. I jumped up screaming, "Dirty O, Dirty O! You did it, not Bernice. You did it!"

Dirty O stopped in her tracks, turned to me and said, "What do you mean I did it?" I reminded her of the time she sent me to Red John's to pick up her package. I told her I had stolen two bags of dope from her that day and shot them all by myself. I told her how I would watch closely every time she allowed me to see her and her friends shoot up. I watched and I learned. Suddenly Dirty O fell to her knees crying, "I'm sorry Denise, I'm sorry I let you see me. Don't turn out to be like me, please! I'm so sorry." Sadly, Dirty O's plea fell on deaf ears. We were no longer mother and daughter; she had become my friend and hustling partner, and I had gotten far too comfortable with shooting drugs to stop just like that.

Not only did I plunge wholeheartedly into drugs and crime, but it wasn't long before I began to be sucked in by the excitement of the gay lifestyle. I met a woman named Carol; she was five feet, six inches tall with a vivacious body. She grew up in Pill Hill and had ultra-feminine characteristics, but her weakness for heroin and freaky sex led her to the projects, and to me. Carol was twenty-two years old, ten years older than me. Her nickname was "Head-Hunter" because of her knack for turning young, green studs like me out to oral sex. Her skilful bedroom acrobatics soon convinced me I was in love. Carol used my affection for her to bait me into performing oral sex on her. "If you truly love me, baby," she would say, "then you would do the same things to my body that I do to yours, and that way I can be exclusively with you and not go out with anyone else to be satisfied. You know I love you, don't you, baby?"

Obviously new to the game and ignorant of the strategies used by pros like Carol, I assumed it was okay to refuse her offer. Convinced that I would not be good at oral sex, I offered an alternative of just being friends. That is when I learned there was another side to Carol. Her sweet, baby-doll voice changed into that of a cold, ruthless thug. "Man, what do you think this is? I'm not trying to be your friend. You know what I need! Now look, you give me what I need or we can't be together no more, period! It's time for you to grow up. What you gonna do?" So I became Carol's sexual protégé; a blob of gullible clay in my sculptor's beguiling hand. The alluring seductress molded me into her sex slave and I learned how to soothe her lusts by mastering the art of oral and anal pleasure.

As I continued in my new lifestyle, my appetite ascended to new heights. Now it was me who drooled like a dog hunting for new partners, looking to mark my territory. Nevertheless, I was new to the game and easy prey, especially for Vivian, Dirty O's current live-in lover. She was twenty-seven years old and always had her eyes on me. Whenever I walked by, she would stare at me like a chained dog lusting at a thick, juicy steak. It was only a matter of time before she decided to take a bite. When Dirty O would leave the apartment to run errands or hustle up some money, Vivian would corner me and mutter all sorts of inappropriate things under her breath. "Mmm, Denise, you gonna be some kind of stud broad" was her favorite line.

This went on for a little while until finally she stopped playing games and made her move. Vivian started sneaking out of their room and into my bed in the middle of the night, when she was sure Dirty O was asleep. She would slide right up on me, pressing her body against mine, and then kiss me. I liked it. "Denise, I told you you're going to be some kind of stud."

One particular night, while Vivian was preparing to perform oral sex on me, Dirty O walked in and she snapped. She snatched Vivian out of the bed and beat her like I had never seen her beat anyone before. She was merciless, pounding Vivian's face until it puffed up like a buttermilk biscuit. I sat in terror as I watched Dirty O kick and stomp her repeatedly until I finally yelled out for her to stop. To my surprise, Dirty O stopped, looked at me long and hard, then turned back to Vivian. "Get up out of here!" she told her. "Go get in the room and don't come out!" Vivian picked her naked body off the floor and dragged it to Dirty O's room. She looked like a tattered rag doll, hair all over her head, limping back to her place of confinement. When Dirty O heard the bedroom door close, she turned back to me and I just knew it was my turn to get jumped on. Oddly, she stared at me long and hard then walked out, slowly closing the curtain behind her.

I cried myself to sleep that night. I always wondered why Dirty O just walked away. That wasn't like her; she didn't let anybody mess with her, especially me. She always took every opportunity to let me know she was in charge. Looking back on it now, I suppose she felt bad about exposing me to her lifestyle. No doubt Dirty O couldn't stand seeing me taken advantage of that way because it brought back memories of when she was taken advantage of as a child.

Vivian stayed around the house long enough for her bruises to heal, then ran off the first chance she got. However, Dirty O wasn't inclined to let her go so easily.

When she discovered that Vivian was gone, she had eyes all over the city looking for her. Less than twenty-four hours after Vivian left, Dirty O received a tip disclosing her whereabouts.

"Come on, Denise. Let's go get her." On the way, Dirty O gave me clear instructions about what she wanted me to do. "I'm gonna knock on the front door, but you go around to the back. If she tries to get out, don't you let her...or else." My heart was beating fast and I was all geeked up.

Just as Dirty O thought, Vivian ran out the back door. But surprise, surprise: I was standing there. "Where do you think you're going?" I said to Vivian, grinning from ear to ear. "Go ahead, run. Run!" I told her, while at the same time yelling for Dirty O. "Dirty O, here she is! Around back!"

"Uh-uh, don't do this; let me go. You know Dirty O is gonna kill me. Don't do this, Denise." By this time, I had grabbed Vivian by the collar of her coat. She struggled a little so I let her go, but as soon as she started running, I yelled. "Hey, Dirty O, there she goes. She's running down Maypole, trying to get away."

"Catch her, fool," Dirty O yelled back. Dirty O was trying to keep up with us, but she kept sliding on a thick layer of ice. "Catch her, Denise, and don't let her get away!" I chased after Vivian until we ended up at a dead-end street and she had nowhere left to run. I barricaded her behind two garbage cans while waiting for Dirty O to catch her breath and get there. I was still grinning.

"Come on now, Denise, why you doing this, baby?" Vivian pleaded, frantically looking around for somewhere to hide.

"Hey, she gonna kill me if I don't do it."

When Dirty O finally came around the corner, she was slipping and sliding on the ice in her plastic cowboy boots. When she got to where we were, she steadied herself and fired on Vivian. She couldn't beat her like she wanted to because every time she swung at Vivian, her feet slipped from beneath her, causing her to almost fall on the ground. I laughed harder and harder every time she slipped. Dirty O kept telling me to shut up, but I couldn't. That was a real comedy show. I laughed until I couldn't laugh anymore.

Finally, Dirty O gave up and settled for the few good licks she had already gotten in. Frustrated, she grabbed Vivian by the arm, dragged her back to the car and shoved her inside. While driving Vivian down to *Eddie's Lounge* on Madison and California, to turn a few tricks before the night ended, Dirty O was mumbling and cursing under her breath, getting louder and angrier with each word. "Woman, you taking me through too many changes. Now you trying to mess up my money. You're mine, you hear me?" Dirty O said, looking Vivian straight in the face. Then, out of nowhere, she began slapping Vivian repeatedly. I could feel the sting from where I was sitting in the back seat. "You ain't going nowhere, you hear me?" Dirty O was holding the steering wheel with one hand and Vivian's neck with the other. "And if I ever catch you so much as looking at my child, I'll kill you!" Vivian didn't say another word and Dirty O put her eyes back on the road. A few weeks later Vivian ran off again and we haven't seen or heard from her since.

*   *   *

Now that all of my cards were out on the table, I had to find a way to fund my habit. My friends and I got together and devised a scheme to get drugs from medical centers. Bernice, Smokey and I would go through the projects collecting public aid green cards. Although the cards were for those in need of medical attention, we collected and used them for profit and pleasure, never medical purposes. It was profit when we sold some of the drugs and pleasure when we used the leftovers for our own recreational means.

At dawn, we would hurry into a line at the medical center on Madison and Racine. Using the stolen medical cards as identification, we were given numbers by various doctors at the center, which we would later use to collect bottles and bags filled with what were called "T's and Blues." The "T" stood for Talwin, a potent pain medication similar to morphine, and the "blues" were Pyribenzamine, a sedating antihistamine. Mixed together and injected, these two drugs produced a high similar to heroin and cocaine, depending on how it was mixed. The street name for this type of high is 'speedballing.'

We would place our orders at the medical center around nine o'clock in the morning and in a short time our numbers were called systematically. When the pharmacist behind the window called our number, we walked up to the window and retrieved two brown bags, each containing one-hundred pills. Afterward, we headed over to Madison and Western and sold the "T's" for a dollar each and the "Blues" for fifty cents. Any remaining pills we used ourselves.

My need for drugs increased, and because drugs were so readily available, I began using more and more. I was becoming a full-fledged junky. I was hustling any way I could. I devised another scheme to bring in some money.

I would wait for the old, drunken mail carrier to come and deliver the mail. Then I would sit on the table in the hall and watch him put the food stamps and public aid checks in various mailboxes. My brain worked just like a computer; there were over two hundred mailboxes, yet I was able to remember which ones contained checks and food stamps. Once the mail carrier left, I went outside to the boxes, raised the template with my thumb, and took out the checks and food stamps. I would then cash the checks at the grocery store and trade the food stamps for money. Almost every cent I got went to buy drugs.

As my addiction grew, so did my criminal behavior. I had no respect for life or the people that were in and around me. I taught my cousin how to steal and we broke into homes, stealing and selling everything we could find to fund my next high. But it wasn't just about the high, I was angry and nothing mattered to me. I didn't care. I had to let my frustration out somehow, so I took it out on society. My little brothers and sisters were at home sleeping on milk crates, with nothing to eat. Nobody seemed to care about that, not even our mother. So I didn't care either. I didn't care when I stole bedspreads, sheets, and pillowcases right off my victims' beds. I felt justified. Life wasn't fair. That's the message it sent me. Therefore, I did what I had to do; I was providing for my family. They had a need; I took care of it.

When Grandmother learned of my criminal activities, she was grieved. "Denise, I expected better of you, baby. Why are you out there in the streets like that? Your granddaddy and I taught you better. Your granddaddy went to work everyday. Now here you are, running around with your momma doing I don't know what. Come on back here with me and your granddaddy," she said. I could feel Grandmother's love pulling for me, but the streets were calling my name.

Grandmother continued to grieve as she observed my steady descent into a low, hellish lifestyle. Every time she turned around, she was hearing about something I had gotten into or someone I had robbed. Every time she saw me, I had a new scar, a new cut or a new gash somewhere on my body. Grandmother continued to plead with me, but all of her love and concern fell on hardened ears. "Denise, how do you think this is making me feel?" she would ask. I continued to resist Grandmother's pleas until she grew very angry and gave me an ultimatum. "Well, Denise, if you don't want to come back home, act like you got some sense and straighten up, don't come here no more because I can't take all this frustration." Grandmother began to cry. She took her glasses off and wiped her eyes with the bottom of her apron, but it didn't do any good: the tears were flowing hard. I had never seen my Grandmother cry like that. Grandmother wiped her eyes again, then put her glasses back on. "Why are you wasting your life? All I ever asked you to do is finish school, and I told you I'll buy you a new car when you finish." I didn't answer Grandmother, I just stood there with my head hanging down, ashamed and feeling bad about making her cry. When I didn't respond, Grandmother seemed to give up on me. "Go on. If that's what you want, go on and stay out there with Annie Mae and all those hard-looking women she be with."

It broke my heart to see Grandmother crying and hurting over me like that, but it wasn't enough to get me to stay or change. Therefore, I took the only part of her advice I could: I left.

And if it seem evil unto you to serve the LORD,
choose you this day whom ye will serve...
Joshua 24:15a

DJ

9

DESCENT

My life began spinning out of control. I had no purpose or direction. I was twisted and savagely wild, like a jungle beast. I did not belong in the world in which I was caged. There were rules, but I was unruly; the world had laws, but I was lawless. I needed to defile, to defy. This world trapped me in a meaningless existence. Driven to color it blue, I painted over the injustice with my justice. Streetology was my justice. All for me and none for you, that was my justice.

I began spending weekends with my cousins on 65th and Stewart. On Friday and Saturday nights, we would hang out at Englewood Skating Rink. My sexual preference was common knowledge on the street, but I tried to keep a low profile because I didn't want word getting back to my Grandmother and other family members. My cousins, however, had front-row seats to the full-thrust arena of my lifestyle. They were fully aware that my sexual appetite was reserved strictly for women, but that did not stop them from continually trying to match me up with male partners. There was one guy who liked me named Willy, but the feeling was not mutual. I was fearful of experiencing sex with boys for several reasons. On top of the other negative

111

impressions I had of men, I once overheard my teenage cousin having sex with a teenage boy. She was screaming and begging him to stop, but he continued violently taking her virginity. I remembered all the rapes that took place in my mother's house during her weekend parties and I was sure that men were not for me. I equated men with pain and doggishness.

Although I was still somewhat inexperienced in the lesbian lifestyle, I was rapidly gaining ground. I was fresh meat in the marketplace and the women were lining up for a choice cut. "Come here you fine, young thing. I've got to have you," I would hear them say.

"Shoot your best shot and go for what you know," was my standard reply. Like penny candy in the neighborhood grocery store, I had a variety of women and young girls to choose from, but I wasn't serious about any of them. I had other things on my mind, like making money. I couldn't make money lying up with women all day. I was a businessman and before anything else, I was married to the hustle. However, my success in the street and with the women made me cocky. I was too young and immature to have the kind of clout I was gaining on the street. I didn't know when to stop, or when to back down. I always pushed the envelope, and it wasn't long before I ended up getting arrested.

One night, a few of my running buddies and I were walking down the street in Rockwell Gardens, trying to find something to get into when we walked up on a police car with the lights flashing. I looked in the back seat and recognized a friend of mine. I walked over to the squad car to ask why my friend was being arrested. The police officer looked at me and said, "Young man, get away from the window. Step away from the car."

"Get away from the car for what?" I said. "I'm just asking a question. I know him; I was just asking you what he did. Can't I ask a question? You mean it's a crime to ask a question now? Isn't this America?" The police officer kept telling me to back away from the car, but I wouldn't listen. "Young man, this doesn't concern you. Now, for the last time, step away from the car." I still didn't budge. I kept going on about my rights and how I could ask a question if I wanted to. Before I knew it, the police officer grabbed me and pinned me against the car, his forearm lodged under my neck. "How old are you, young man?" the police officer asked. Coughing through his chokehold I replied, "Old enough." The police officer backed up and put his hand on his billie-club. "Now, it's obvious you are stupid and don't understand what you are doing and who it is that you are talking to, so I am going to overlook your stupidity and ask you one more time: how old are you?"

I looked around at the growing crowd. All eyes were on me. I could feel my knees buckling and sweat creeping past my hairline onto my forehead, but I couldn't let them see me sweat. "I'm eighteen, so what?" I said with a smirk. I was only sixteen, but if I had to go to jail, I wanted to go to the adult lock up, and I knew you had to be eighteen to go there.

"Well mister, your fat mouth just earned you a night in the lockup," the police officer said, reaching for his handcuffs. I gave the crowd one more glance. All eyes were on me. *You better not cry*, I thought to myself, clenching my teeth together. I was getting sick, I could feel the rumbling down in my belly. *Will I fold like an easy chair or represent like the ambassador that I am?* I wondered myself if I would be able to hold up. On the inside I was coming apart. My throat quivered and my top lip started itching. I wanted to bite it, but I let it itch until it burned. I swallowed a lump of air and my throat quivered again. I wanted my mother. Once again, I needed her and she wasn't there.

Because my reputation was on the line, I had to be cool and act as if nothing bothered me. I drew a deep breath through my nose, cocked my head to the side, stretched my arms out in front of me with my two fists clenched together and stared at the police officer, as if to say, "Cuff me, fool, cuff me." I turned to my cousin and gave a quick wink and a half-smile, letting him know that I would be back. Jail was just another road to travel.

It didn't take long for me to learn that jail is a horrible place. Being young and still new to the gay lifestyle, I had no idea what kind of persecution and ridicule gay people suffered. Out on the street, my tomboy appearance was a plus because it gave me more pull with the ladies, and more respect from some of the straight guys. In jail, it was another story. The guards teased me about my masculine appearance from the time I arrived. In the morning, while waiting to be processed out, I heard one of the guards joking with another guard saying. "We got us a real live bull dagger back there, wearing Fruit of the Loom briefs." Their laughter echoed through the hall and back to the cells. I felt so embarrassed. When it was time for my release, I stepped out of those briefs and left them right there on the cell floor. I remembered my uncle saying to me one time that a woman could be in the gay life, but didn't have to dress or look like a man. Sadly, I knew that, in spite of the persecution I would face for being a stud, that's what I was.

After my release, I stood naked in the bathroom mirror looking at my body and thinking how deformed it was. From head to toe, it was all wrong. *How could I be born this way?* I thought to myself. *I'm all messed up; my body is deformed, looking like a female with breasts, a vagina and a large rump. I'm a man! I was meant to be a man.* I did everything in my power to change what was wrong with me, trying to make it right. Like a rattlesnake shedding its seasonal skin, I peeled off my young, tomboy image and took on the appearance of a real man. I strapped down my breasts with an Ace bandage. I pulled it and wrapped it until I was as flat as a board. I had my afro shaped then streaked black and blonde at the barbershop. My shirt was the perfect fit; it went well with my three-piece denim outfit. I became the epitome of masculinity, right down to my Fruit of the Loom underwear. And to top off the new look, I covered the unwanted hole between my legs with my freshly acquired strap-on penis, purchased from an adult store on the north side of town. It was the perfect fit.

Who Said It Couldn't Be Done?

I was ready to hit the streets. Cool as a '57 Chevy, I was ready to do a little cruising, shoot a little dope and ride life until the wheels fell off. It was my time now; it was time for me to sit back and enjoy the scenery. I had changed; just like the seasons, just like my mother. Yeah, I was The Man.

No longer an inexperienced teenager, I began meeting hard-core studs like Scary. I met Scary thorough Cathy, Dirty O's ex-lover. I considered Cathy to be a mother figure. She was with us for so long that I had grown quite fond of her. Even after she and Dirty O broke up, I would visit her from time to time. During one of my visits, Scary was there. When I introduced myself as Denise Jones, Scary looked at me strangely and said, "Man, you've got to change that name." When I asked, "To what?" she replied, "DJ," and we hit it off just like that. Scary and I grew very close. She showed me how to be a player, and it wasn't hard to master the game. In her exact words, I was a quick study.

We started hanging out at Den One Lounge, a speakeasy on Rush Street where the gay crowd hung out. This is where I tried out the new skills Scary taught me. She and I, along with some of our other friends, were there regularly on Wednesday nights. On Fridays and Saturdays, we went to Helen's Lounge on 75th and Kimbark. There I met all kinds of people and loved the selection of women, especially women like Jackie. Jackie was one of the finest young women on the set at the time. Just like a lioness stalking her prey, I laid back in the cut, waiting for the right moment to make my move. One particular weekend, I had a light buzz and was leaning against the bar with my sunglasses on, drinking slow-gin and orange juice and getting into the music. I was a little disappointed that I didn't see Jackie until suddenly a sweet voice whispered in my ear. "So how long are you going to wait to ask me to dance?" I knew right away that it was Jackie and I smiled.

"I was waiting on you, baby. I figured when you got tired of these little boys and was ready for a real man, you'd step to me, so I waited." I turned to face her and she smiled. I melted like ice in a glass.

"What's your name?" she asked.

"DJ," I replied.

"DJ, hmmm, I like it. I'm Jackie," she said, looking me up and down. "So tell me, DJ, why are we still standing here?" I could tell by the look in her eyes and the sultry tone of her voice that dancing wasn't what she had on her mind. I adjusted my collar, grabbed her hand and proceeded toward the door. I passed Scary on the way out and told her I'd catch up with her later. Scary saw what I had on my arm and gave me a nod.

After that evening, I was mesmerized with Jackie for a minute, but the magic began to lose its power and it wasn't long before I was back it the marketplace looking for the next best thing. After leaving the lounges, my friends and I would go back to one of their apartments in Rockwell Gardens and party some more. We called it The Gay House, and we'd be dancing, drinking, getting high and wrapping up with our women until the sun came up. I was no longer content with just one woman. I always scanned the pastures seeking a lonely heifer. Scary would constantly say, "Man, what's up? Why are you always messing with other men's women?" But I played it off, like the women were coming on to me.

Laughing and joking, I said, "Man, I don't know what you're talking about. You know how the women are when it comes to me: they can't get enough. I beat them off with a fly swatter, but they keep on coming. You want some? Come on, man, take your pick. Which one you want?"

Scary replied, "You better stop playing around, DJ. I'm for real. Some of these straight guys around here are getting tired of you. You need to slow it down, man. It ain't no joke out here, man. This is the streets. You hear me, man?"

"Go on with that mess, man. You just jealous. I already told you to take your pick."

"See man, you keep on playing. I'm for real, DJ, just watch your back, OK?"

"Yeah, alright man," I lied. I wasn't thinking about what Scary was saying or what anybody else thought. I kept doing what I wanted to do.

Eventually, I ended up right back with Carol. During the time we were supposed to be together, I started messing around with her best friend, Marsha. I got so into Marsha that I bought her a ring, and Carol found out. She came over to my house and before I knew it, she grabbed me and had me hanging outside of the twelfth floor window, daring me to mess around on her again. My feminine baby-doll turned butch on me once again. While dangling outside of the window, I was pleading for my life. "Baby, I love you," I yelled, loud enough for the people down on the street to hear. "I love you, nobody else, just you. Please, please," I begged. "I PROMISE, I won't deal with nobody else. JUST YOU! You know I don't care nothing about her. She ain't nobody. I PROMISE; nobody else; JUST YOU! I LOVE YOU, ONLY YOU!"

Who Said It Couldn't Be Done?

After crying and begging some more, she finally pulled me back inside the window. I was so embarrassed; I felt like a punk. That night the little boy in me became a man. I vowed I would never allow anyone to control me the way Carol had done. I was supposed to be her man, but she proved to me that night who really wore the pants in our relationship. I felt something break inside of me. I became callous and unfeeling. My emotions were hardened and every drop of tenderness was gone. I promised myself that nobody would ever run or rule me again.

After that incident, Carol and I began drifting apart but we were still territorial. I didn't want her to have anyone else and she didn't want me to have anyone else, which is what set the stage for our next bit of drama. I caught Carol in bed with some young stud from the neighborhood. I didn't interrupt; I waited patiently until they finished and then jumped on the stud. She was easy; she didn't even fight back. Now it was Carol's turn. There wasn't going to be a repeat of our last fiasco. I was a man now and I wasn't going to be disrespected. Carol kept trying to explain her way out of it, but I wasn't listening. Because I wasn't listening to anything she had to say, she tried to flip the script and get mad at me. I wasn't falling for that one either. It was a violation when I messed around

121

on her, but now she wanted to justify her actions, as if the rules had somehow changed. I had taken all I was prepared to take. She kept trying to talk and I wouldn't let her, so she tried to swing on me. Now, I have to admit that I was a bit nervous; Carol was no joke. Although she was a woman, she was as strong as a man and, as much as I hate to admit it, I was scared of her. I hadn't forgotten how she dangled me out of the window of my apartment and was able to pull me up by her own strength. However, this was about my manhood. She had already put the word out about how she had whipped me that night; now I had to fight to get my honor back. Before I knew it, I drew back my fist and swung on her with all my might. I hit her in the eye and knocked her flat out. Despite the fact that Carol and I were no longer officially dealing with one another, that's how things were back then; she was mine and I was hers.

Finally, enough was enough and it was time for me to move on. All my days and nights revolved around the streets: hustling, getting high and snuggling up with my women. I continued shooting heroin, drinking cough syrup and dropping pills. I befriended another hype named Dino, who was just as desperate as I was. To finance our assorted addictions, we committed smash-and-grab thefts. When a car would be stopped at a traffic light, we would throw a slug through the passenger-side window and grab any purse or bag on the seat near the shattered window. Then we'd split the money and go buy cough syrup. We thought we owned Western Avenue near Adams and Jackson, and along Cicero Boulevard. We played those spots until it got too hot and Dino came up with another plan to steal merchandise from the back of moving trucks. Dino would ride the backs of trucks from Lake and Western down to Western and Van Buren, breaking the sliding door open. He would hastily throw boxes of goods out the back; I would have other people gather whatever boxes they could and run. Sometimes we would even hit freight trains for merchandise such as BB guns, gym shoes and coats. We would then sell the items for cash and head back to the dope spot.

Another hustle was playing checks and credit cards. I would telephone the police and report that someone was firing a gun into an apartment. When the squad car arrived and the police got out to investigate, I would throw a brick or pellet through one of the squad car windows and steal the police officer's ticket book. Then I would write myself out tickets, which I used as identification to cash stolen checks and use credit cards.

Who Said It Couldn't Be Done?

I was a traveling hustler. Every time one location got hot, I would move to another spot. Having mastered all four corners of Chicago, I began to get bored and search for new friends and places to hang out. Wherever I smelled money, that's where I would make my mark. This time my new hustling spot became the Double Doors Lounge on Damen and Milwaukee Avenue, along with a few other taverns along that strip. I also began hanging out around the Pierce Apartment Building on Damen and Pierce Street. It was there that I met some of the craziest people I would ever come to know.

I ran into an old dope fiend named Marilyn, who I knew from Helen's Lounge. She was a prostitute and lived in the Pierce apartment building with a young Hispanic pimp named Carlos. We hooked up and started getting high together. She introduced me to her sister, Janice, and her two brothers, Lil Melvin and Big Melvin. These guys thought they were hard-core pimps and dressed in jump suits, platform shoes and wide-brimmed hats, like Super Fly. I also met a prostitute named Karen, who lived in the Pierce apartment building with her man Blue, who was a drug dealer. The scene around there was so scandalous that one night another hooker bit a piece of Karen's nose off out of jealousy, because Karen was the new "chocolate" woman on the set who was getting all the attention.

Everyone had developed their own line of business; mine was robbing tricks. After the two sisters lured tricks to the apartment building and performed their sexual acts, I would wait in the hallway and rob the tricks of their jewelry and money as they left the apartment. I would then sell the jewelry and take the money and buy dope.

There was also a woman named Big Cheryl who lived in the Pierce apartment building. Big Cheryl sold heroin, T's and Blue's and rented used works (needles). Her spot was a shooting gallery and all kinds of people hung out there. It appeared that Big Cheryl had been using drugs for a long time. Her entire body was so badly infected that deep abscesses had scabbed over so thick in some areas her skin was hard and rough, like a brick. Sometimes I would see her take a syringe of dope and stab herself in the arm, leg or hip, or sometimes she would get someone to hit her in the neck because she had no usable veins left.

When I look back on it now, it is amazing to me that I survived that sick lifestyle. I was around people obviously as sick as Big Cheryl, but we all continued to share the same needles, cookers, water and eyedroppers.

We would clean syringes with the same bloody water that other individuals had used to shoot up. Sometimes we would shoot the dirty water on the walls or the floor and just continue to draw up dope and shoot it. It didn't matter so long as we got high.

*   *   *

My life continued skidding downward. The individuals and environment I was attached to abounded with craziness; all around me people were losing it. Everybody was frantic. Anyone who looked like they had something – money, jewelry, or whatever – was fair game for a stick-up. It got so crazy we began robbing each other and called it, You Snooze, You Loose. It was in this atmosphere that I first met Crazy Leon. At that time, I had no idea why they called him Crazy Leon, but I soon found out.

Leon and I hooked up and worked closely to develop a routine for our robberies. We would hide on the third floor of the Pierce apartment building and wait for tricks to pass us on their way to the fourth floor, where all the prostitutes hung out. We would then jump out on the tricks before they reached the fourth floor, pull out our guns and stick them up. If they refused to hand over their valuables, Leon would threaten to make them jump out of the window. He actually made a few jump, but not before claiming their goods. Leon was a wild man. One of the things that helped him earn his reputation was the sword he carried with him at all times. He once used it to cut off the penis of a man who had money hidden in his rectum and refused to turn it over when Leon demanded. I would be terrified when he would perform these vicious acts. He was so crazy and treacherous that I thought he would kill me, if I told him I didn't want to take part in this type of madness. Around that time, I began to realize that my life was out of control. Eventually Crazy Leon went to the penitentiary and I got word that Marilyn had died from an overdose of drugs. I figured that was a sign for me to leave the scene, so I did. Several months later, I returned to Pierce Street and discovered that our old spot had been closed down and boarded up by the City of Chicago.

I met a drug dealer named Craig who invited me to try some Tac or PCP (Phencyclidine), which is a "dissociative" drug (meaning it distorts your perception of sight and sound and can cause hallucinations). Craig invited me to snort as much Tac as I wanted at no charge. I suppose I realized there was an ulterior motive to his generosity, but despite my instincts I took him up on his offer. Shortly after I took a few snorts, he made his move and tried to rape me. My own fear of rape, mixed with the affects of the PCP, made me so crazy that I scared Craig off by snarling like a wild tiger while fighting him off. Craig got away from me as fast as he could. After watching him flee down the alley, I managed to stagger to a snack shop and buy a glass of milk to help bring me down from my high. Not only did that experience make me not want to use PCP again, but it also made me suspicious of Pierce Street, so I returned to my old hang out on North Avenue and Damen.

Like a hungry lion, I resumed prowling the lounges down Damen Avenue near Belmont Street and eventually met a blonde-haired prostitute named Pisces. She was bisexual and was dating a man called Wild. When Wild went to jail on a burglary charge, Pisces and I hooked up. Nine months later, Wild was released from jail and when he heard that Pisces and I were dealing, he went berserk. He stormed over to Pisces' house and kicked in the door. "Pisces!" is all he said and I started shaking. His voice seemed to rattle the walls. When he burst into the bedroom, I had one leg in my jeans and the other raised midway, ready to slip into my jeans. He stood there for a second staring at us, then turned to Pisces and charged toward me like a raging bull. Ordinarily, I would have taken my chances and fought any man who competed with me for my women, but I didn't dare try it with Wild. I saw in his eyes that he was much crazier than I could ever be. Swiftly, I turned and made a mad dash for Pisces' bedroom window and in one leap, I jumped from the second floor all the way down to the ground. I ran down the street with only one leg in my jeans and the other pant leg in my hand, but I didn't care: I was free. While Wild was trying to climb out of the window after me, Pisces bolted out of the front door and made her escape. Knowing that we couldn't return to Pisces' apartment, and with nowhere else to go, we moved in with Dirty O in Rockwell Gardens.

Things worked out well between Dirty O and us. We seemed to get along just fine. We did everything together. After hustling, we would go back to the apartment and shoot up or skin-pop each other in the arm or in the hip. We skin-popped because there were times when we couldn't find a vein to shoot the drugs in, so we stuck the heroin into our skin instead of our veins.

In the summer of 1978, after living with my mother for about a year, Pisces got an apartment at 500 West Oak Street in the Cabrini Green housing project. In order to supply our habits, Pisces and I returned to our old stomping ground on Damen and Milwaukee Avenue to work our hustle. Once, while Pisces was in the process of turning a trick with an undercover police officer, I and a few other individuals had planned to rob him. As we began committing the robbery, a police car was driving by and observed some fighting going on. That officer must have called for back-up and soon there were police cars coming from everywhere. When I heard the sirens and saw all the flashing lights, I took off running. Realizing there was nowhere to go, I hid underneath a parked car. I began to wonder if I had exhausted God's Mercy. So many times He had spared my life, but I kept on doing my own thing. Perhaps by now, He had had enough of me.

The police officers were searching the alley and found me hiding under the car. As they pulled me out, my whole body was shaking from fear. Though the alley was dark, I could see murder in the officers' eyes. One of them pointed his gun in my face and told me not to move, or even breathe, or he would blow my brains out. Another slammed me to the ground, handcuffed me and told me he had half a mind to kill me right there, but was going to take me in and book me instead. They took me to the police station on Grand Avenue, where I was charged with another attempted robbery. Fortunately, the case was dropped and I didn't go back to jail.

Who Said It Couldn't Be Done?

Not long after that, I met Michael. Michael was a dope fiend and a hustler. Michael taught me how to pop trunks, which was one of the smoothest hustles I had ever learned and kept me out of jail for quite awhile. I made it my full-time job. Sometimes I would make two or three trips a day to Maxwell Street to sell stolen merchandise. I found everything in those cars except a dead body. After the merchandise was sold, we would split the money three ways, return to 500 West Oak and get high. One day while we were getting high off of T's and Blues, I had my back turned toward Pisces lighting a cigarette and noticed a moving shadow on the wall. Michael was having a seizure. I had never seen anything like that before. I was so scared that I chewed up the unlit cigarette and stood there shaking; I thought he died. Pisces hollered for me to get some ice and a spoon. She told me to put the ice under his testicles and she put the spoon in his mouth. He lived, but from that point on I refused to get high with him when he shot T's and Blues.

I heard there was a new drug out that could get four people high off of one pill. The drug was for people with cancer and those who suffered from chronic pain. A woman in a house on the corner of Clybourn and Sedgwick was selling the pills (Dilaudid) for twenty dollars, so I bought one. Parked in the parking lot of Jenner Elementary School on Oak Street, I broke off a small piece of the pill and using my cooker and water, cooked it up and shot it. That small piece of pill was so powerful that I couldn't tell my hands from my feet. It reminded me of the first time I shot heroin. It made me feel like I didn't have a care in the world. I introduced Pisces and Michael to the woman that was selling the pills, and soon the woman could not keep a steady supply because all the shooters heard about it and burned the spot out.

Pisces and I began to distance ourselves from one another. We were hustling and get high buddies, and sometimes she would become a booty call. During that time, I met Audrey, an alcoholic and cough syrup fiend. Audrey and I started hanging out and drinking cough syrup together and soon became lovers. I had stopped shooting Ts and Blues and was no longer shooting heroin, but I was drinking cough syrup and popping pills (591J, 529 and Wheelchairs) with Audrey nonstop. Drinking syrup was the going thing at that time. We would sometimes buy a half-gallon of syrup and cut it with Lightning to stretch it, in order to make a profit.

Sometime when I would drink syrup and pop pills, I would drink coffee to boost my high. I discovered that drinking a hot liquid like coffee immediately after taking the syrup and pill combination would get me high faster. Often the coffee would be the only food substance we had the entire day. We weren't interested in eating because food wasn't a priority among addicts.

Since Pisces and I were no longer on good terms, I started kicking it with Audrey more and more. Life became one big rush to get high. Prior to meeting me, Audrey had been dating a man named Smoke. They broke up and Smoke moved in with another woman, but when he heard about us messing around , he put the word out that he was going to kill us. One night when Audrey and I were so high that we couldn't make it home, we stumbled onto a small playground with a merry-go-round and ended up spending the night there. As we sat there, passed out in each other's arms, Smoke just so happened to be passing by on his way to work and spotted us. He could have killed us, but instead he just left us there. Clearly God shielded our lives that night.

Pisces and I continued to have sex every now and then, but mainly we hooked up for business purposes. She was always bringing something new to the table. One day she persuaded me to break into her neighbor's apartment in the 500 West Oak Street building, to steal some lottery money her neighbor supposedly had won. Pisces said she found out there were several thousand dollars stashed away somewhere in that apartment. They were nice neighbors and I knew them, but that did not stop me from breaking into their apartment. I carefully planned just how I would break in. However, to my surprise, when I arrived the keys were dangling in the door. The neighbor's children arrived home from school early that afternoon and had forgotten to take the keys out of the door. I grabbed the keys and banged on the door loudly, trying to scare the children. When I heard them screaming, I busted in and there, standing before me, were two children with wide, frightened eyes. I made them go in the back room and close the door. I didn't wear a mask, thinking the children would not recognize me. However, when their parents returned, they informed them that their next-door neighbor had robbed them and their parents immediately called the police. After questioning the parents, the police came to Pisces' house to investigate. Pisces always warned me that if she couldn't have me, no one else would either. So she ratted me out to the police. The lottery winnings were a set up. It was her way of getting back at me for cheating on her with Audrey.

Who Said It Couldn't Be Done?

I was taken to the Belmont and Western Avenue police station and booked for robbery, home invasion, and assorted charges for tying up the children and holding them hostage. The District Attorney's office offered me thirty to sixty years for the charges to run concurrently. I refused to take their offer because I learned that the parents of the children had refused to press charges against me, requesting only that I get counseling for my drug addiction. The state, on the other hand, was not willing to let me off that easily. I received 90 days in Cook County Jail and four years felony probation. Considering my sentence could have been much more severe, God was still showing His Mercy to me: a two-bit, low-life, broken down dope fiend.

I met a cutie pie named Queenie while serving time in Cook County Jail and still maintaining my relationship with Audrey. I was really tired of dealing with no-good women, but I was stuck. When I got out of jail, I started seeing Audrey, but I didn't want to deal with her because I planned to hook up with Queenie when she was released. I was torn between Audrey and Queenie, but more importantly, God was still dealing with me to come out of the lifestyle I was living but I was stubborn. Fortunately, His Mercy was covering my life.

Who Said It Couldn't Be Done?

One night I had a dream that troubled me. I dreamt that some vicious black cougars were determined to devour me alive. One bigger cougar ate all the smaller cats up. The big cat kept trying to get at me and looked angry. The dream troubled me so much that I woke up early and went to morning service at *True Holiness Deliverance Ministry*. There I shared my dream with Presiding Elder Mosley and he gave me the interpretation. He said that the woman I was dealing with was setting me up to be killed. It sounded pretty wild, so I didn't believe it. When I made it home, Audrey was there waiting for me. I got a little nervous when I saw her and really didn't want to be around her, but she wouldn't leave and kept begging me to go home with her. Finally I went, thinking it was the only way to get rid of her.

I ended up spending the night and the next morning, Audrey woke me up and asked me to go to the store for her. Something about the whole thing just didn't seem right. At first I told her I wouldn't go, but when she kept pressing me about it, I got dressed and walked out the door of the apartment. The hallway was dark, and as I turned to go down the stairs, I heard clicking sounds coming from behind me so I took off and ran down to the stairwell at the other end of the hall. Even then, I still could not believe this woman was trying to get me killed.

As I returned from the store, Audrey was hollering from the tenth floor window, "DJ! Don't come in the building! Smoke is gonna kill you!" All I could hear was Elder Mosley's voice and the interpretation he had given of the dream. From that point on, I never messed with her again…it was OVER!!! God was still showing His Mercy and Love for me. What a Loving God!

Months later, God allowed me to go back to jail for thirty days on a theft case. While in jail, I reconnected with Queenie. She was released one Friday, and when I got out the following Sunday, she was there to pick me up. We checked into the Michigan Hotel, got high and began to exchange game. I learned all about Queenie. She was a professional booster, whose specialty was stealing Ultra suede suits and fur coats from *Lord & Taylor* and *Neiman Marcus* stores in Woodfield and Golf Mill shopping malls. She introduced me to a new line of business called fold, wrap and stuff. For this hustle, I wore a long riding skirt and a girdle, and then would go through stores taking merchandise off the hangers, folding it up and stuffing it inside the girdle. The riding skirt was wide, so nobody could notice the items stashed underneath. I felt awkward wearing a skirt, but since we were making money hand over fist, I didn't mind.

The more money we made, the more we shot up. We were living life to the fullest, or so I thought. Queenie was the best thing going at that time and I was crazy about her. She had the looks, the body and most of all, the money. She was sweeter than candy and all about me. When Queenie caught another theft case and was sent to the penitentiary for four years, I tried to wait for my good thing, but my drug habit would not allow me to. I ended up returning to North Avenue and hooking up with some of my old partners, Mae, Chocolate and Tanya, who were professional pickpockets. Together we developed a hustle that involved prostitution and robbing tricks. Pretending to be prostitutes, we would lure potential customers (or tricks) to alleys or secluded gangways. Our asking price was $15, but this was only a scam to see how much money they had in their wallets. The moment the tricks produced their wallets, we would pull them towards us and pick their pockets, or sometimes cut their pockets completely off with a razor blade. Then we would snatch anything in their hands, shove them away and run. We did this whole procedure so quickly that most tricks didn't realize what was happening to them until we were gone. After we escaped, we would split the money and go our separate ways.

I had descended to the point that there was nothing I wouldn't do in order to get high. My addiction led me to some of the most decadent drug addicts and dope fiends imaginable. Some had holes in their bodies and open abscesses into which they would pour in the dope. Sometimes they would put the needle in veins within the open abscesses and shoot in the drugs. Others would screw off the syringe, leaving the needle in their arm, and cover the spot until the next time they were ready to shoot dope. This wasn't the life I desired or dreamed about, but it was impossible to imagine living any other way. I suppose at some point I surrendered to the thought that I would die the way I lived, a miserable dope fiend.

10

HEROIN STREET

I searched hard for Euphoria but could not find her. I searched for her on every street corner and in every alley, but she was not there. I was told that she was at the pool hall just around the way. I ran as fast as I could and paid everything that I had, but she was not there. I begged for her daily. I brought her many gifts – other people's rent money, my rent money, Grandmother's rent money; children's bikes, pictures off other people's walls, fur coats, leather suits, jewels; women for her to lay with: Mother's women, my women; car stereos, stolen checks, food stamps, credit cards – because the stakes were high. I gave her my arms, my legs, my breasts, every vein daily, until I could give no more. She ravished my toenails, pulling them off one by one. She was not satisfied until the red blood ran and yellowish-brown puss formed a thick, crusting scab. She smiled at this, even laughed. When my toenails found the courage to resurface, she snatched them off again. I gave her all these things because I needed to see her smile.

Nevertheless, Euphoria swindled me. She stole my beauty, my youth and my health. At nineteen I was old. My hair was thinning like an old man and my health was failing. My bones ached, I was cold in the summer and coughed all year long. When I coughed, my stomach heaved up the blackness of smoke soot, and sometimes it burned. This morning, just as yesterday morning and every morning before, she incarcerated my thoughts. Euphoria was my first thought every day and my last every night. I was loyal to her, though she was disloyal to me. Just once more, Lovely Lady, I beg you: satisfy me tonight. Have mercy on me. Show your lovely face this one last time.

With two large packages of heroin in my hands, I prepared to meet Euphoria. I entered into a familiar spot, a rundown shooting gallery. I dragged myself over to a corner where a urine-stained mattress was lying. I dropped myself onto the mattress and continued to hold the purchase in my hand. I was shaking. I was cold.

I thought about some of the happier times in my life. I could see Uncle Ivan brushing tears from my face and telling his Top Cat that everything was going to be okay. I saw myself walking proudly down the street with my humongous afro puffs propped up high on top of my head. When the memories ended, a half smile and half frown surfaced upon my face, and I firmly held the freshly acquired packages in my hands. *Why me?* I thought to myself. *Why did my life turn out this way? Why did Uncle*

Ivan have to die? Why couldn't Uncle Ivan be my daddy? Where is my daddy? I want my daddy. I want my mommy.

My misery ached in me hard, like a big piece of wood lodged in my chest. Deep inside me, I could feel a knot. There was no space left, just a knot. I looked at the heroin clutched in my hands again. I ripped open the package, pushed my face into the cake and took two quick breaths. I didn't move, I just sat there, waiting for Euphoria one more time, but she did not come and I was sick.

More memories came. Grandmother and I were outside hanging sheets on the line. The smell was so fresh and crisp. I still remembered the feel of her large hand rubbing across my tiny face. I smiled and she smiled, and we continued to hang our laundry. I missed my Granny.

Slowly, I tore open the other heroin package with both hands and slammed my face hard into the floury powder. Tears and blood came and my nose burned, but Euphoria was not found. More tears came; they flowed hard. They made yellow mud of the cake on my face and neck and much of the heroin still in the package. To die would be peace, but there was no peace for me. Every day I lived in the dark prison of life. Life was my sentence without Euphoria.

Who Said It Couldn't Be Done?

I pushed my hand down in my pants and pulled out my *Seagram's Gin* pouch. As I drew the works from the pouch, my stomach began to turn. I was going to lose my bowels, but I held them and went through the ritual of cooking the drugs to shoot. I wiped tears from my eyes, pulled my belt off my waist and prepared to tie up. I beat, rubbed, poked, and squeezed my arm, searching for the tiny passage. "Come on, come on," I pleaded.

More tears came when a small vein rose to the surface. My arm was numb, but I could still feel the crave. I bit my lip, pushed the needle in, and pulled the plunger of the syringe back. No blood came. Hastily, I removed the needle and whipped my arm some more looking for another vein. *Not now! Not now! Come on. Please...please. I need a hit! I'm sick! Come on, man. I need this.*

I shoved the needle back in my arm and pulled the plunger back. I squealed as the deep red stock mingled with my brown sugar. Inhaling deeply and then exhaling, I took my time and carefully shot in the healing mixture. *Aaaah!* A cool breeze rose up from my arm and through my throat, preparing me for Euphoria, but she remained elusive yet again.

I often wanted to commit suicide. Life, and the cruel reality of it, was something I no longer wanted to deal with. I deliberately tried to overdose several times, but each attempt failed. Since God wouldn't allow death to have me, having no other choice I continued to do what I did best: get high.

*   *   *

I was drawn back to North Avenue and Oak Street, like metal drawn to a magnet. I drove forward with my life, pushing the pedal all the way to the floor, but I was low like a gas needle wavering back and forth on empty. I hooked back up with my old flame Pisces and went back to hustling.

"Pisces, give me the perforator. You are moving too slow. You must not want to get out here and make this money. Now, come on, we got to go make this money, man."

"Shut up, fool," Pisces said. "You always got something to say. Just stamp the checks evenly this time. Line em' up right. The last time you stamped the checks all crooked and we almost got caught."

Counterfeiting checks was a lucrative business. We printed fake checks using a perforator we stole from a warehouse on Division Street, then stamped them with a rubber stamp. Bob, one of my business partners, was my runner. He cashed the checks at a currency exchange where the employees knew him. I didn't mind working with Bob; he was a fair guy and only charged a small fee for the run. The only problem was I had to meet Bob at a lounge downtown on Wells Street to pick up the money, and I had no wheels at the time. Getting downtown sometimes presented a problem.

One day, I introduced myself to this other hustler named China and offered her $25 to take me down to Wells Street. She agreed, but after we cashed the checks, I ended up giving her half of the money because I liked her. That's how China and I became friends. Once a week, China would take me to meet Bob at the Wells Street lounge to make the transaction. It was easy money.

China was involved with a woman named Bobbie at the time, and of course, I had my woman Deon. Deon spoke three languages fluently. China and me pimped our women together on North Avenue and Damen, and sometimes on Rush Street. We would go wherever we could to make money. After the women finished working, we would double up at a nearby motel on 35th and Michigan Avenue. Because we were so deeply into drugs, we needed more money than what the women were bringing. China and I would meet during the week at the juice spot, share a bottle of syrup and drop some 591j pills.

That would get our motor running and we were off to the rat race, pick-pocketing, popping trunks and doing whatever we could to feed our addictions. Eventually, I went back to jail for violation of probation. Because it was dangerous for a prostitute to work the streets of Chicago without a man, Deon returned to her previous pimp because she claimed she couldn't work the streets as a renegade.

When I got out, I tracked Deon down, threw her in the car and drove to 31st Street Beach. "You see that lake? I will suffocate you and drop you over in there if you ever call yourself working for another man! Don't be messing with my dollars, you hear me?" Soon I went to jail again for prostitution and Deon was gone for good.

Fresh out of jail, I met Mia: booster by day, prostitute by night. Mia was born and raised in Peoria, Illinois. Mia was working as a renegade at this time, so I became her pimp-lover. This was not an easy relationship. Mia was fine as long as we were shooting up, but every once in a while she would have crazy thoughts about taking my money and running off to get high on her own. The drama between us escalated when we moved into the Michigan Motel on 35th Street and Mia started running off regularly. I would go and find her, beat her, drag her back to the motel and have sex with her.

146

One afternoon we had a conversation while I laid on the edge of the bed watching television. Mia walked up close to the bed and pushed her body real close to mine. "DJ, why you not talking to me?"

"What you want Mia? Can't you see I'm trying to watch *My Three Sons*?" Mia pushed away from the bed and backed up in front of the TV, blocking my view altogether.

"DJ, you love me, don't you?"

"Mia, would you please move from in front of the TV?"

"Come on, DJ, listen to me. You know how I know that you really love me?"

"Alright. Turn the TV off. What's the matter with you now, Mia? Do I need to go get you some more blow? Or do I just need to stomp you through this floor?"

Mia stood there with her eyes fixed on me and I began to calm down. "OK, Mia, I'm sorry for getting mad at you. Come here and tell me how you know I really love you."

Mia quickly forgave me for being so mean to her and immediately began explaining her views on love to me. "Well okay, if you insist. I know that you really love me because every time I run off, you always come find me,

147

bring me back home and tell me I belong to you. Am I right?"

"Yeah. Sho you right. You my ho and I own you, and don't you forget that."

"Quit playin', DJ, I'm serious."

"Alright, baby. But you are mine. And I ain't sharing you with nobody."

"I know. And there is something else I know, too."

"And what would that be?"

"I know you only beat me because you love me so much and you be missin' me when I run off, because you be wantin' me home with you."

"You right again. But tell me something, Mia. Since you so smart and know all of this stuff, why you always taking me through all these changes? Why can't you just stay put and do what you supposed to do and make this money? Why can't you just act right? Huh?"

"I don't know, DJ" Mia said slowly. "I'm sorry."

A few weeks later, Mia and Brenda, one of China's women, ran off together for four days. I called Gloria, a close acquaintance of mine, to ask if she had seen Mia.

"Well, I haven't seen her, but she on her way over here right now to get her drugs and her working girdle."

I knew Mia would eventually make her way to Gloria's apartment so that she could retrieve her works. Mia couldn't go too long without a fix. I asked Gloria to stall Mia until I could get there and she agreed. Mia didn't show up that day, so I spent the night and was awakened by a quiet whisper early the next morning. "DJ," Gloria said, "Brenda's at the door."

"Alright, alright," I whispered back. "Let me hide. I'm going in the back room where Mia left her kit. Don't let her back there until I close the door." When Brenda entered the room, I stepped from behind the door with my fists already clenched. "Tell me where she is, and you better not try to lie."

Brenda denied knowing Mia's whereabouts, so I gave her one more opportunity to tell me, but before she could fix her lying lips to say anything I punched her in the mouth. Her lip began to swell and blood ran from the side of her mouth. She crumbled like rotten wood and began blabbing. She told me that Mia was downstairs the car with James, parked on the side of the building. James was our regular driver who usually took us hustling. I told Brenda to stay put until I got back upstairs.

Like a lion, I spotted my prey sitting in the front seat of the car with her head leaning back against the

149

headrest. Stealthily, I crept up on the passenger side of the long, sleek antique Cadillac and launched my attack. I snatched on the passenger door but it was locked. Startled by my unexpected presence, Mia screamed. When she realized it was me, she cried out, "Oh no! James, go, it's DJ! He's gonna kill me!!

Before James could stop shaking long enough to turn the key in the ignition, I jumped on the hood of the car and threatened to kick in the windshield if he tried to pull off. I guess Mia wasn't worth the cost of a new window because James got out of the car, walked around to the passenger's side, opened the door like a chauffeur, smiled at Mia and gave me a nod. I yanked Mia out of the car and James quickly sped off.

I beat Mia from the curb on the side of the building all the way up to the third floor to Gloria's apartment.

"Didn't I tell you if you ran off again with my money, I was going to show you just how much I loved you? You thought I was playing with you? I told you, don't you play with my money!" We ended up going blow for blow in Gloria's kitchen. I was still pounding fist to face when I finally realized that Mia was no longer fighting back. She was propped up against the wall like a rag doll and wheezing heavily. I could hear her lightly muttering, "I promise, I promise I won't run off anymore, DJ. Just stop beating me. Please don't kill me."

I didn't hear Gloria's children screaming in the background, or Gloria and Brenda yelling hysterically for me to stop. As I slowly returned to a state of sanity, I looked around the kitchen and began to shake on the inside. The damage I had done and the way I snapped frightened me. Was I really the tornado that had swept through this room moments ago? The table was broken, chairs were turned over and broken plates and pots were everywhere. I had knocked a pot of spaghetti off the stove and Mia and I both had blood and spaghetti all over us. There were three giant holes in the door from when I swung and missed Mia. My knuckles were swollen and bore many cuts and scrapes, though I didn't feel any pain. The eye of the storm had passed.

I reached in my pocket and pulled out a knot of $100 bills. I scraped several off the top and handed them to Gloria to cover the damages. I told Mia to go clean herself up and threw her a few bags of dope to ease her pain. Later that night, I took her back to the stroll to make my money. Her face was swollen like a biscuit, her right eye was almost swollen shut, and a couple of her ribs were fractured, but I didn't care. She had stolen four days worth of my money and I needed my money.

Several months later, Mia ran off for good. We were still staying in the Michigan Motel at the time and without Mia to pay the rent, I soon fell behind. The money I made hustling every day covered my high, but nothing else. I managed to hide out from the motel manager for about a week until she cornered me early one Saturday morning and called me into the office. When I couldn't produce the money, she called the police. I tried to get away before the police arrived, but they caught me outside the motel and arrested me for trying to leave without paying.

My life continued on a perpetual cycle of hustling and getting high. I had to step up my hustle to keep my high going, so I roamed the streets day and night looking for every opportunity to feed my addiction.

Who Said It Couldn't Be Done?

In my life I have traveled down many roads
and have been too many places,
carrying burdens by the loads.

At the intersection of Talwin Drive
And Pyribenzamine Street
I had a gala of a time,
Oh what a feast!

On Cocaine Lane
Nothing was boring or plain.
And In Gay Town
I would sho' nuff get down.
But happiness I never found.

On Prostitution Row, my, how those women could go!
But nothing could compete with the scene on Heroin Street.

But then I ran into a Dead End
Someplace I had never been.
I looked around and God showed me a way,
A straight gate where I could escape.

The gate had a sign that said "JESUS"
And beyond was a highway called
"The Way of Holiness."

So I made up my mind to go and see
What this JESUS could do for me.
                    Written by Denise Jones

11

SPIRITUAL AWAKENING

"Hey, look over there. Ain't that that niggah DJ?"

"Naw, that ain't that mark, man. That's not him."

"Naw man, that is him. I know that drunk fool anywhere. Look at him, stumbling all over the sidewalk about to fall. I know that's him. I can't stand that mark, man. He ain't nothing but a wannabe. How is this fool out here getting more women than we get? I can't believe this fool out here getting *my* money. I'm gonna kill that niggah."

"Pull up over there. If it's him, we got something for that punk."

They were three men I knew from Rockwell Gardens. I had a few run-ins with them in the past, but I didn't think it was anything serious. I had no reason to think they had anything against me. We went our separate ways and left each other alone.

They eased up to me in a brand new 1980 Cutlass Supreme and let down the driver's side window. "What's up, DJ? We ain't seen you in a while, where you been?"

"Hey, what's up? I'm just out here, man. Hustling and making this money." My words were slow and dragged out of my mouth. I stumbled closer to the car and leaned over on it to keep from falling on the ground. When I got my balance, I stretched my neck so that my head was in the window looking inside the car. The driver leaned away from the window and, looking at his friend in the passenger seat next to him, began fanning his hand back and forth to beat off the foul smell of my breath. My vision was blurred, but I saw the third thug lighting up a joint in the back seat.

"I like your ride, man, this is nice. Who is that in the back seat? Man, let me hit that. Hey, why don't y'all run me to the dope spot? I'll take care of you. I need a few more bags of blow and some syrup."

"DJ, you crazy," the driver said. "You make it sound almost like you been looking for *us*; well, you found us. And we sho' been looking for you."

The person in the passenger seat started laughing again. "Yeah, DJ," he said. "We been out here riding around trying to find you. Matter of fact, we was just talking about you. It's a stroke of genius that we happened to run into you like this, man." He smiled slyly, looking over at the driver.

"So, where you heading?" the driver cut in. "Which spot you wanna' go to?"

"Man, if y'all just take me to the dope spot out west on Washington, I got y'all," I said, patting my shirt pocket to indicate I had gas money.

"Get in, fool," the driver shot back. "You high already and still trying to get high. DJ man, you wild." They all started laughing again, even the thug in the back seat.

I climbed in to the back and melted into the plush leather seats. The soothing smell of new leather and the slick sound of the music put me in a real mellow mood. I slid down low and let my head lay back on the headrest, listening to what the driver had playing in the cassette deck. Before I knew it, my head dropped and I was in a deep nod.

Usually when I nodded, I was oblivious to the world around me, but I was acutely alert when I heard the driver fussing. "Man, look at that mark. I ought to kill this dyke right now, messing up my brand new ride and slobbering all over himself. Man, I ought to pull over right now and shoot this mark!"

The guy in the passenger seat chimed in. "I can't believe he out here pulling more women and making mo money than we making. Man, that's *our* money. Check his pockets," he said, motioning to the thug in the back seat.

"What he got? Git it all. How he gon' walk around with *my* money in *his* pocket? Check his pocket, fool."

By now, the driver was really getting riled up. "Come on, let's take this fool out for messing with our money."

"Naw, naw, man," said the thug in the back next to me. "Check this out, man. Y'all want to hear something wild? What you think about this? This little mark wants to be out here like he own the streets. Now, do y'all know about the *Brach's Candy Factory* just up the way? Let's take him around the back of the building and show this punk what a *real* man is all about. Man, my thang is hard anyway," he said as he began to rub on himself. He continued, "Let's rape this fool first. Maybe we can straighten him out; let him get a taste of a real man before we take him out of his misery."

"Yeah. . .yeah! That's a good idea. I get to go first," the driver said, with a wicked smile.

"Yeah, he looks like he need a man anyway," the thug in the passenger seat said. I could hear all three of them laughing. Through the power of the drugs, God allowed me to listen as they planned to kill me. They were laughing and talking about me as if I was nothing, like I wasn't even there.

"Yeah, man," the thug in the back seat, said. "This niggah thinks he will disrespect me and I ain't gon do nothin' about it? Man, hurry up and get to this candy factory; I'm gonna blow this fool's back out."

He started rubbing on my thigh and my skin began to crawl. My stomach twisted into knots and I needed to throw up, but I feared they would kill me on the spot if I moved, so I swallowed deeply and held it in. I could feel cold tears welling up in my eyes, but I held them back also. I remained motionless. I had no movement at all except for my fuzzy thoughts. I didn't know what to do. I pretended to be in a deep nod, but my terror was mounting. I needed to escape, but I didn't see how. I was trapped with the enemy. My palms began to sweat; my finger tips were stinging. I scratched lightly on the leather of the seat while slowly inching my hand closer to the door handle. The thug next to me continued to rub my thigh. I wanted to turn to him and beat him to a pulp, but I knew I couldn't beat all three of them. I had to sit there in nauseating disgust while he pulled my leg open so that he could slide his hand all the way up my thigh. He pressed against my vaginal area through my jeans and began jabbing me with his fingers.

"Yeah," he said. "I'm a make this punk squeal like a little pig. He think he's a man, but when I am done, he's

158

gonna know what a real man is. Hurry up and get to this factory; I can't wait to get a taste of this sweet thang." He kept jabbing his fingers at my crotch area trying to penetrate me, but my strapped-on penis was in the way. When he realized what he was doing, he hollered out, "This man got a penis like I do. Aw no...we got to kill this mark!"

My terror escalated and my heart pounded faster and faster. I could feel more cold tears welling in my eyes. It occurred to me at that point that this was how it was going to end. As I thought about my body being found mangled behind the candy factory, I realized that God was allowing me to hear their plan through the power of the drugs. *Oh God,* I thought to myself, *help me!*

As we approached the traffic light at Lake and Kildare, very slyly, I scanned the car to see if I could make a dash for safety. The thug next to me had taken his focus off me, but was still trying to penetrate me with his fingers while masturbating himself with his other hand. The other two were involved in conversation in the front seat. *This must be my escape,* I thought. *Should I jump out and run away? What if they shoot me in the process? What if I don't make it? What if they catch me?* My mind was blown. I couldn't believe this was happening to me. When we stopped at the red light, I jumped out of the car and ran as fast as I could. The car hadn't come to a complete stop, but I didn't care, I just jumped out and ran. As I ran, I kept listening for the gunshots and bullets that were going to bury themselves in my back. I kept waiting to die and wake up on the other side of life.

The thug across from the driver jumped out after me. His feet seemed to hit the pavement much harder and faster than mine did. Those cold tears finally came down my face and blurred my vision, but I had to keep moving. I was terrified, but I couldn't look back. The driver threw the car in reverse and swiftly backed down the street, trying to get close enough for the thug in the back seat to pull me back into the car. My heart was pounding in terror, pounding faster and faster as I ran. I couldn't let them catch me. Memories of what I had seen men do to women began to bombard my mind. I've seen women tied to cars and dragged down the street, then left cut-up and bleeding right on the edge of the street, like a bag of trash. I've seen women raped by men, have trains pulled on them, beaten over the head with wine bottles, yelled at, embarrassed, injected with drugs and left for dead. I hated men. I had hated them for a long time, and the thought of one touching me to have sex with me made me sick to the stomach. I would rather die than let them violate me.

Men took my mother from me. They made her cold and stoic. It's their fault that my mother left me by myself when I was just a child. My momma loved me and she would have stayed with me and been a good mother, but she believed those men – all of them – when they said they loved her and would take care of her. But there was no one to take care of her, and she did not take care of me. *Mommy, where are you? I need you. Help me, Mommy! Don't let these bad men get me, Mommy. Mommy, I'm scared.* But my mother was nowhere to be found. I no longer had a mother. The person I knew as my mother no longer existed. All that was left was Dirty O, and all Dirty O was about was abusing and pimping women, just like any other man. I didn't fit into his life at all, so he threw me away, like the women tied to those cars.

My pursuers closed in on me like a hunter closing in on prey. With nowhere to run and in total desperation, I turned abruptly and jumped through the two-inch-thick glass door of an old apartment building a few feet in front of me. As I jumped through that thick glass, all I thought was *kill yourself DJ, kill yourself. Don't give those bad men the satisfaction of defiling you and crawling all over your body. Kill yourself before they kill you!*

Unaware of the stares and cries of the building's occupants, who had emerged from their apartments at the sound of the shattering glass, I stumbled up to the second floor. With blood gushing like a fountain from many places on my body, and my hand severed almost completely from my wrist, I heard a voice yelling, "Oh my God, get some towels! Call the police!" That was when I looked down and realized my request had been granted: tonight I would die.

As the minutes pressed on, I became more and more incoherent. It was getting dark, and I found it hard to breathe. *Hey, what's going on?* I said to myself. *Why can't I see? Why is it so dark in here? Where am I? Who turned out the lights?* I wanted my mother. *Mommy, I beat em'. I beat the bad men. They didn't get me. The bad men didn't get me.* As life oozed out of my limp body, I was suddenly afraid, more afraid of death than of the bad men who were pursuing me. I didn't want to die after all. I wanted to live. *Oh, God, what have I done? God, if you spare my life, I will live for you, please don't let me die like this!*

Vivid images of my childhood ran through my mind. It was just as I'd heard, my life flashed before me. I saw myself in the living room of our apartment in the projects when I was ten years old. I was pretending to be a preacher. I wrapped myself in an old sheet, preached, and sang my heart out to my little brothers and sisters that day. The song I sang was *Lord, Don't Move My Mountain* by Inez Andrews.

I was seeing more and more how I had made the wrong choices for my life. *Oh, God,* I thought solemnly. *Don't let me die out here in the streets like this; please let me live. I'll change; I promise, I'll change!* As I slouched weakly against that wall, undoubtedly dying, my lifeless body slid to the flood and landed in a pool of my own blood. Objects around me continued growing dim and hazy. Life was fading out, but not before I remembered Ruthie Jordan. Because Ruthie did not own a car, she sometimes asked me to drive her to service at *True Holiness Deliverance Ministry* on Friday nights or Sunday mornings. Ruthie often told me that God had a very special purpose for my life, but I wasn't trying to hear all of that at that time. I told her, "Naw, that's for you old folks. You had your fun and now you want to settle down. Well, that's fine for you, but it's my turn and I'm not missing any of my good times. God is for you old holy-rollers, not me. Y'all need God; I don't need Him."

Who Said It Couldn't Be Done?

I remembered the last time I saw Ruthie, preaching to a group of teenagers around Rockwell Gardens. She looked right at me and left me with these powerful, prophetic words, "Young lady, the day is coming when you are going to need God and you will call on Him, for He will be the only one able to help you. When the storms of life come and you find your back up against a wall, then you will call on Him."

This was that day; my bloody back was up against a dingy wall. Life had beaten me down, just as Ruthie said it would, and now her words resounded in my ears. I began to call on God. "Help me, God. Help me, Lord Jesus! Lord, if you spare my life this time I will live for you!"

The police arrived and once I was laying in the backseat of the squad car, I passed out completely. When I revived, the staff at Loretta Hospital was asking for my name and telephone number. I was able to mumble my phone number but couldn't get out my name, which they ascertained from a tattoo on my arm. Somehow, the hospital was able to get in touch with Dirty O. I remember hearing them tell her there was nothing more they could do for me there, so they were transferring me to Cook County Hospital, where she could identify my body. At that time, my mother was pregnant with my youngest brother

Jermaine, and the news was so upsetting she went into premature labor and was rushed to St. Luke's Presbyterian Hospital. My Auntie Mable ended up coming to see about me.

When I arrived by ambulance at Cook County Hospital, the emergency room doctor immediately took charge and began ordering blood transfusions and stitching my wounds. My arms and shoulders were split open, I had a gash in my head, and my hand was barely attached to my wrist. The staff at Loretta Hospital had given up, but God gave me another chance and I lived.

I underwent surgery and awakened in intensive care, bandaged from head to toe. When the doctors were through sewing me up, I had one hundred and eighty-three stitches holding my tattered body together, and not one of them was stitched to my broken heart. All I could do was lay there and cry. I laid in that hospital bed, feeling beaten down and wanting to die. I could feel the terror I felt that night, being chased down that long, dark street. I could still hear those heavy footsteps, rapidly pounding against the pavement behind me. Why did that happen to me? What will I look like when these bandages come off? These scars will be with me forever. Every time I look in the mirror or bathe, I'll see them, like a memory in time etched in my body as permanent reminders of that night.

When I was dying that horrible night, I promised God that I would change, but the longer I laid there pondering all that happened to me, I knew I wouldn't keep that promise. I couldn't think about God; wrath was stirring inside of me and I needed revenge. I imagined my violators laughing and talking about what they tried to do to me, as if it were a joke, but it was not a joke to me. Why should they laugh while I mourn? I began to conjure up ways to get even. I wanted to bring them close to death by breaking their spinal cord with a bat and then watch them suffer. I wanted to paralyze them enough so that every inch they rolled in their wheelchairs would remind them of what they had done to me.

As I laid there conjuring up acts of revenge, I recalled my Grandmother quoting scriptures and saying, "Vengeance is mine, saith the Lord," but I couldn't wait for God's vengeance. I wanted my own vengeance and I wanted it soon. Although I looked like a mummy all bandaged up, the bandages did not stop me from shooting T's and Blues and heroin. I was miserable and drugs were the only thing that could take me out of my misery and numb my pain. Scary shot the drugs in my feet for me, and although my feet would swell up like water balloons, I kept on shooting. Once the stitches and bandages came off, I had to take physical therapy for almost six months due to the extensive muscle damage in my hands. I focused all my energy on healing and regaining my strength so I could carry out my vendetta. While I was still plotting my revenge, my sister ran into the house one afternoon and told me that one of the men who chased me was killed in front of the twenty-five fifteen building on Jackson Boulevard. I knew God did not kill him, but hearing that one of the culprits who had tried to kill me had died a terrible death affected me, so I just let it all go.

I also forgot all about my vow to God that I would change. Instead of honoring my vow to live for Him, I played God like He was some hustler I ran up on in the streets. I went right back to living the way I was used to living, hustling and making money. About a month or two later, I was up on the north side and ran into China. We went and picked up some drugs out west on Chicago Avenue and got high. While waiting for our drugs to kick in, we went to the tavern and shot some pool. When the tricks started coming in, we picked out a mark who wanted to spend some money and told him we would take care of him. Once we got him outside in a compromising position, sex was not what we had in store for him.

"China, tie his hands tighter, man. We can't let him get loose."

"DJ, would you shut up! I know what I'm doing. I am pulling this rope with all my might; this is a big man. He must be part gorilla. I ain't never seen no hands this big and hairy before."

"If you move, you big ape, I am going to pull this trigger and blow your brains out. Stand there and don't move cuz' I can feel my trigger-finger itching right now. Let my guy tie your hands tighter; I want them to turn purple, you hear me, purple! China, hurry up. He is about to chew through the steel of my pistol. You thought we was gon' let you put them monkey balls on us? Man, you must be dumber than you look. You the dumbest trick we ever beat, man. China, you through with his hands yet?"

"Yeah, man, I think I got them tied tight enough. He's gonna die wrapped around this pole." China began rummaging through his pockets and came across a fat knot of folded bills. "Jackpot! Oh-oh DJ, let me see. We got one, two, three, four, five, six hundred, seven…DJ, this gorilla must have a good job. Eight hundred, nine, ten, eleven, twelve, thirteen, fourteen, fifteen…I didn't know apes could work in America. Thank you very much; you just donated $1,500 to the 'Save an Ape Foundation.' Just for that, we gonna let you live."

"Come on, China, let's get out of here. You know it's only gonna take him about thirty-five, forty minutes to untie himself and I don't feel like shooting no monkeys tonight. Let's go so this fool can make it back to the animal kingdom."

We hit the jackpot! Laughing our heads off, we were on our way to pick up more drugs. After shooting the drugs, we went to shoot pool at the Double Doors Lounge. When the pool balls began wavering, I knew it was time to go. We went back to China's house to get high some more and chill out for the night.

Usually when I got high, my sex drive got high with me and whatever woman I was with was in trouble. Since China and I had been hanging out making money, I didn't have a female handy who could gratify my sexual impulses. Feeling a little restless and very horny, I decided to go out and cop some more dope and head home to my girl, Shirley. It seemed like that would be my life forever, hustling and getting high. It had been all I'd known for as long as I could remember.

Who Said It Couldn't Be Done?

As I was walking across someone's backyard, a vicious dog came charging out at me. I took off running until I ran into a tall fence. I tried to climb over, but the fence was tall and a little damp, so I couldn't pull myself up. Finally, I made it to the top and flipped over, but the wires that stuck out of the fence caught the palm of my hand and ripped it open. I was so disgusted. I went down the street fussing and cussing because of what that stupid dog made me do.

I stumbled over to the CTA station on 35th and State Street and rode the "L" downtown, where I transferred to the West Congress line heading back to the West Side. While I was walking down the platform, my walk decreased from a slight weave to a drunken stagger. Eventually I stumbled a little too close to the edge of the platform and fell off, landing only a few inches from the third rail. The third rail of the tracks is electric, and to touch it usually means death by electrocution. As I laid there unconscious, God mercifully held the train back until the police arrived and rushed me to Mercy Hospital. When the doctors revived me, they told me I had overdosed.

I should have been dead long before the third rail incident, yet despite having reneged on my vow to change my life, I was still alive. In my mind, I heard echoes of

Ruthie Jordan prophesying about how God had a work for me to do and how much He loved me. I began thinking that maybe God really did have a purpose for my life, because no matter what I did to kill myself, I wouldn't die. What reason could He have for rescuing me from the clutches of death, time and time again?

Still driven by Ruthie Jordan's prophecy, I found myself attending services at *True Holiness Deliverance Ministry*. The storefront church I visited years before with Ruthie had relocated to Halsted and 104th Street. Over the course of four or five months, I visited Friday evening and Sunday morning services to hear the Word of God. As a child, I occasionally listened to radio preachers from time to time and heard about the Ten Commandments and The Great Flood, and I remembered the songs *Lord, Don't Move My Mountain* and *Sweet Home*, but I had never heard anything like what I was hearing at *True Holiness Deliverance Ministry*.

On Sunday mornings, Presiding Elder Donald Mosley would teach as if it were his last time. I admired him the first time I laid eyes on him. He was strong and powerful, yet gentle and kind as well. He was a man of great principles, who lived what he preached and taught. I saw in him what I longed to see in every man: true

171

leadership and compassion for people. He also had a great sense of humor and usually the entire congregation would be rolling with laughter as he taught the Word of God. I marveled at the way the little children sought his attention. When their classes walked beside the pulpit on the way to the restrooms, they made sure they waved at him. It didn't matter if he was in a fiery part of his lesson, whenever he saw one of the children wave, he always waved back and smiled. I liked seeing the children treated so kindly. However, despite all of this, Elder Mosley made me nervous. I wasn't used to his kind of man: a *real* man. He wasn't afraid to get in someone's face with the truth of the gospel. He kept it real, and I wasn't ready to hear the truth about me.

On Friday evenings, God would lead Elder Mosley to call various aspiring ministers to preach. One Friday night, I was as high as helium and kept wondering why I was back there again. Elder Julius W. Collins happened to be preaching from I Corinthians 6:9-10. Elder Collins is a man of average height and a slender build. He has a delightful personality, and his wide smile frames perfectly aligned teeth. His message was clear and straight to the point, and although all of my thoughts were slurred, that preacher hit me as if I was an amateur in a professional boxing match.

"The Devil comes to steal, kill and destroy!" he thundered. "The gay life, drugs, oral sex and fornication will keep you bound, but you may not realize it until it's too late. You think you are having fun, but deep down you are miserable. You've been crying all week long because your life is on a road leading nowhere. You've run into a dead end and it's time to change your course. Why don't you give your life to Christ?"

Elder Collins stared me down as he preached. It seemed he had watched a video of my life. How did he know I had been crying all week long, looking in the mirror at how old and rundown I'd become? I was only twenty years old but I looked and felt fifty. My bones ached and my feet were always swollen; I was tired all the time and my teeth were pulling away from my gums. I was dried up, with black spots on my face and abscesses on my arms and legs. I had no food, no home, and nobody to love me. I was nothing, nothing at all.

That minister's message grabbed me by my jugular, but I was stubborn. Despite the knot in my throat, I continued slumping in my seat and rode it out until service was over. Then I went back to the west side, hustled up some money to get high and tried to drown out the Word of God.

Another Friday night, Elder Melvin Dwayne Patillo was preaching the Word of God. Elder Patillo had been delivered from one of Chicago's most notorious gangs, and was a former dope fiend. He talked about his life on Jackson and Pulaski and shooting T's and Blues every day. He used to have to wear an old firefighter's boot because his feet were swollen from shooting drugs. I sat there attentively because he was talking my kind of language. We had something in common. He preached from the Word of God with ferocious fearlessness and didn't miss a beat. Everything he said was right on the money and applied directly to my life, yet I sat there, hard as a brick and cold as nitrogen. So once again, I left that service just as I came: without God.

Periodically I would follow up on my thoughts about God, but the thought that Jesus could be the solution to the madness in my life faded from my mind. Each time God's Salvation was presented to me and I resisted, my life got worse. I was spiraling out of control, but my stubborn pride wouldn't allow me to admit that I needed Jesus to rescue me. I slid back into my life of drugs and fornication, just like a chilled hand slipping into a warm glove, but I couldn't deny that after hearing The Truth, life in the fast lane just wasn't the same. Whenever I would go to the drug spot, I would picture Presiding Elder Mosley in my mind, and his powerful words thundered through my memory. All I could hear was the plea to the fornicator, drug addict, liar and dope fiend. His words were haunting. Something kept telling me that this Jesus stuff was for real. God had a grip on me, and apparently, He did not plan to let go.

DENISE

12

MERCY'S CHILD

As the days, months and a few years dragged on, I was getting really tired of my lifestyle and the things I had reveled in for so long. Quite to my surprise, the last person in the world I would expect to help me began pulling on me to be saved and give my life to Christ.

Once again following up on my thoughts about God, I decided to go to a Sunday service at *True Holiness Deliverance Ministry*. When I entered the building, I had to wait in the vestibule for a few minutes until the brothers located a seat for me. I could hear the praises going forth through the doors leading to the sanctuary. When the brothers finally opened the doors to usher me inside, I couldn't believe who I saw dancing in the middle aisle, wearing a beautiful dress, high heels and with hair freshly done. It was the most beautiful sight I had ever seen. My mouth fell open. The tears flowing down Dirty O's face seemed to bury themselves in my heart. She didn't see me; she didn't even know I was there.

Several months prior, Dirty O had given her life to the Lord and joined *True Holiness Deliverance Ministry*, where I had been attending off and on over the last several years. *Unbelievable*, I thought to myself. *Is this for real?*

Dirty O and I had lost contact in the street because of our lifestyles; the deeper we got, the farther apart we grew until before we knew it, a couple of years had gone by and we hadn't spoken. Suddenly I couldn't wait for that service to be over.

Immediately following service, I found Dirty O outside and approached her. "Man, Dirty O, what happened to you? A dress? And what is that you carrying…a purse? Are you for real? Where's your gun, man? Where's your woman? Come on man…What's going on?" I was shooting out questions like forty going north.

"Hello, Denise. It's good to see you, too. What happened to hello? How are you doing? Good to see you? Glad to see your life is not messed up anymore? What about that? Are you sure all you want to know is what happened to my gun?"

"Naw, Dirty O, I'm glad to see you. You know, I'm just not used to seeing you like *this*. Looking like a lady. What's going on?"

"Well, Denise, it's a long story." Dirty O took me by my arm as we began to walk. There were a few more awkward exchanges between us, but we were talking and I liked that. It was good to see Dirty O, although I still couldn't believe what I was seeing. Before we parted ways,

Dirty O told me she had asked Sister Roshell, one of her beloved Sisters-in-the-Lord, to call and follow up with me. Roshell had come out of the street life also, and Dirty O thought she could reach me through her testimony.

It was less than a week later when Sister Roshell and I first talked on the phone.

"Yes, may I speak with Denise?"

"This is DJ; who is this?

"Yes, I know you don't know me and are probably surprised to hear from me, but my name is Roshell. I'm the sister your mother spoke to you about."

"Oh yeah, Dirty O told me about you. It's wild, right? I can't believe it. Dirty O is a trip, ain't he?"

"I'm sorry, but you are losing me. Let's backup for a minute. Dirty O? Who is Dirty O?"

"Oh, I'm sorry. I thought you knew. Dirty O is my mother, you know her as Sister Annie. I can't believe she really has changed. It's different looking at her. It reminds me of when I was little girl. Before I grew up, I saw her looking something like that. So it's alright."

"Wow," said Sister Roshell. "That really is something. If you knew some of the names I was called, and the way I carried on while out there in the streets, you would be surprised about that too! So I can understand."

Sister Roshell and I talked for hours. I liked her right away; she seemed exciting. When she invited me out to visit *True Holiness Deliverance Ministry* again, I told her that I had been there plenty of times and would be glad to come back. However, my purpose at that point was not God; I was trying to work trade. I heard her sweet voice over the phone and now I wanted to view the body and face that went with that voice. I wasn't thinking about being saved, but a sweet honey like Roshell was near and dear to my heart.

The following Sunday I went to service. I paid little attention to the testimonies and the overall service, all I was interested in was spying out the identity of the woman who had called me. Little did I know that she was sitting on the pew right next to me! When Presiding Elder Mosley called for the singers to come to the front, I leaned over and asked my mother, "Where is she? Is she here? When am I going to meet her?" Mother replied, "You'll meet her, just be patient." At that moment, Elder Mosley called for Sister Roshell to come to the front for special prayer because she was going to have an operation the following week. Slowly turning my head to the front, I realized who Roshell was and I thought I would die. I was sitting there getting loud and irritated, trying to work trade in the Lord's House, and the woman had been sitting by me all the time. I knew she heard everything I said and I felt so stupid.

After prayer was administered, Roshell returned to her seat next to me, introduced herself and told me she would call me soon, but that she was on her way home because she wasn't feeling well. The following week Roshell called, just as she said, and told me she wanted me to spend some time with her. Now that was something I had been waiting to hear! The notion of spending time with a good, clean church girl excited me. When she invited me out to one of their morning prayer services during the week, I quickly agreed.

When morning service was over, we went to Brown's Chicken on 111th and Halsted, where I thought I would make my move. As we sat at the table, I was rubbing my legs and opening and closing them, trying to let her know that I was available and hoping that she was, too. At the time, I had no idea this woman was a minister, but it came out during our conversation and squashed all my hopes of having a taste of this "clean, purified woman." I had always heard that if you want a clean woman, go to the church house, but never mess with a minister. *Doggone it*, I thought, *that's that*. Our luncheon abruptly ended.

Roshell continued to call and always invited me out to service, but since I knew I couldn't have her, I'd always say, "Naw, that ain't for me." Disappointed, I went back on the prowl, hustling and getting high. My birthday, November 10, was drawing near and I was making big plans. This was going to be *my* day. All I needed was some good dope and a clean woman from that *True Holiness Deliverance Ministry* to help me celebrate. I laid some rap on a couple of the sweet sisters, but none of them seemed to like what I was suggesting. So I got some drugs and a dirty woman...Happy Birthday.

Everything about my life was contrary to what I knew God wanted for me. I had resisted God every time He reached for me, and had nothing to show for it. I was in my early twenties at this time (21 or 22 years old, I believe) and still in my madness. My perspective on life was twisted, and my view of God was twisted as well. However, the saints steadfastly prayed, and my mother continued to place sisters in my way, hoping to steer me to Christ.

One afternoon, my mother brought a young woman named Harmony by my apartment and began bugging me about going to church with them on Sunday. I declined and repeated my old familiar line, "I'll be back one day." Sister

Harmony immediately laid in on me and told me that if I didn't come when God called, I might come another way, meaning in a coffin. I quickly showed them the door, telling them to let the doorknob hit 'em where the Good Lord split 'em! "Go on back to that holiness ministry where y'all came from!" I shouted angrily, and slammed the door behind them. *Why did my mother bring that skinny girl to my place?* I was very upset at my mother and didn't want any part of what they were offering. I wanted God and my mother to leave me alone.

Quite surprisingly, as time went by, I began missing the praises and the saints dancing in the aisles. So once again, I decided to drop in on a Sunday service. I hung around for a few months or so, just long enough to forget about my insane world. It actually did me some good; just taking a break from the street life was sobering in itself. And those few months were all God needed. His Word began stealthily taking root in my spirit. I could feel myself getting very uncomfortable with my old lifestyle and wanting to live a good life, like the saints at *True Holiness Deliverance Ministry*. I was developing a conscience. Shooting drugs and robbing people did not feel natural anymore. I did not get the satisfaction I had once gotten from it. But old DJ was a diehard. I couldn't grasp the concept of letting God control my life. I couldn't see Him; I didn't understand Him. All I knew was that the change I saw in my mother was real, and I wanted to change too; I just didn't know how to let go. I even stopped using drugs for a minute, but went on pretending to be living a sober life, even after I went back to using drugs and stealing. It was during this phase that I made what could have been a fatal mistake: I stole a television set from the home of a Vice Lord. The Vice Lords ruled the West Side and everyone knew not to mess with them, but I was so strung out that the consequences did not enter my mind until it was too late. The Vice Lords' unswayable vow was to kill me, and they warned my family and friends not to hide me unless they wanted to partake in the brutal beating they had prepared for me. So I was on the run again, sneaking in and out of vacant buildings and peeping around corners. I was tired and miserable and all I wanted was a peaceful night's rest, but I couldn't afford it; I had to keep moving. Some nights I checked into the Viceroy Hotel in order to sleep without looking over my shoulder.

As I wandered aimlessly back and forth, feeling as if all hope was gone, Ruthie Jordan came to mind. So did Presiding Elder Mosley. I remembered the joyful expressions on the faces of the saints as they praised and worshipped God. I remembered their laughter. I could see their smiles and white teeth glistening. I could envision them with their heads thrown back, their arms lifted up high in submission to God. Mostly, I thought about the peace that my mother had finally found. Her rough, manly exterior had been transformed into that of a sweet, tender woman. I saw her wearing beautiful, feminine attire as she joyously strolled from one end of the aisle to the other, worshipping and magnifying God. I could see her throat quiver as she threw her head back and opened her mouth as though she would speak, as a smile as wide as the River Nile slid across her face. "Hallelujah," she'd whisper. "Thank you, Jesus," she would say. "Glory to Your Name, God," and tears of joy would continue to flow.

I longed for such peace. I yearned and craved for it. Deep down inside I knew God was the only way out of my crisis. I knew He was more than just *an* answer, He was *the* answer. It was all coming together like a puzzle. Nothing I was doing seemed to fit: not drugs, women, hustling, stealing, or being on the run. My mother and I had been living the same life, doing almost the same things, yet now she was on a good path. She had tried to get her life together many times in the past, and each try turned out to be a dead end. Now she had given her life to God and was going somewhere. It was as if God was telling me, "Look at how I've straightened out your mother's life; let Me do the same for you."

Early one morning, beaten by my travels, I sat on a fire hydrant on Chicago Avenue and Western to rest. I was as high as I could get and unaware of my surroundings. I didn't know that my mother saw me as she passed by on the bus, on her way to work. At first I thought I was dreaming when I heard my mother calling my name, "Denise. Denise!" I was ashamed for her to see me in that condition, but that was who I was. She talked with me for a moment, encouraging me once again to turn my life over to Jesus, then got on the next bus. Alone again, I started rocking back and forth with my face buried in my hands. "I need You, God," I cried. "I need You as never before. Help me, God" I cried and moaned.

Once again, God's mercy rushed in and rescued me. He honored the prayers of my mother and the other saints, calmed the rage of the Vice Lords and drew me out of the pit of death once more. I came out of the streets once again, intending to serve God…until I met Kim five months later.

*   *   *

Kim was a young woman who had known God at one time in her life, but didn't sell completely out. Like me, she refused to give Him a surrendered 'yes.' We hooked up and became lovers. Kim liked cocaine and introduced me to free-basing. We hustled together playing checks, then copped cocaine and got high. Lesbianism and drugs ruled me. I lost weight until I became skin and bones. When the hustles stopped bringing in enough to cover my ever-increasing habit, I began taking my frustrations out on Kim. As things escalated, Kim turned back to men for sexual gratification.

We would still work together when it was necessary to support our habits. Once we went to the Hyatt Hotel near O'Hare Airport to hustle. We had separate rooms and without my knowledge, Kim called a guy named Rooster to come over and entertain her. I got angry when I found out, even though we were not dealing with each other at the time. We ended up fighting and I beat Kim to a pulp and left her on the cold hotel floor, her face swollen with my fist print and bruises covering her body. Later, Rooster returned to the hotel and found Kim just where I left her and took her to a nearby hospital for treatment. When Kim's grandmother saw how mercilessly I had beaten her, she hired a hit man to kill me. I learned about the contract shortly thereafter through an old acquaintance and came up with a plan to get Rooster arrested on an old warrant. The police went to Kim's grandmother's house and not only arrested Rooster, but Kim as well, for being his accomplice. She was eventually released, but Rooster was not as fortunate.

Still determined to have me killed, Kim's grandmother hired another hit man named Trout. Once again, God allowed me to find out about the hit and I moved to Milwaukee, Wisconsin, hiding out at my play-mother Cathy's house. After about two weeks, I began tracking Kim down and found out she was being held at the Rosemont Police Station for trying to play checks at the Hyatt Hotel. I called the Police Station to find out Kim's court date and showed up on the morning of her bond hearing, sharply dressed in my favorite denim outfit and snakeskin boots. When I saw Kim, her eyes screamed out for help. Her bond was set at $10,000, so I told her to ask the judge to reduce it to $5,000, which he did and I paid it. After her release, we checked into a hotel, shot some drugs and had sex. During our intimacy, we had simultaneous orgasms and it seemed as though my bodily fluids had entered her body. I asked her if she felt what I felt and when she said she did, I thought I had impregnated her. The devil had taken control of my mind to the point of absolute insanity. I actually *believed* I was a man.

Who Said It Couldn't Be Done?

On the other hand, my mother was doing really well at this time. She had gotten married to a saved brother named Michael Freeman, and was pregnant with my youngest sister, Angela. All of the pieces of her life seemed to be falling in the right places while mine were still falling apart. I was mostly amazed at the physical transformation in my mother. All visual resemblance to Dirty O was gone. There were no more pistols tucked in her crotch, no more plastic cowboy boots, and no vodka bottles stuffed in her back pockets. I didn't smell men's cologne reeking through six-day-old sweat. There were no more cigarettes dangling from her mouth. I couldn't believe she was my mother.

When Mother found out about the contract on my life, she was concerned that something awful would happen to me. I didn't quite know how to react to all the concern she had for me. Could I really trust her? Had my prayers for a mother finally been answered? All of the times I looked out of the window into the sky, asking God to bring my mother home; was God answering those prayers at such a time as this? A time that I had long stopped believing would come; a time when it really didn't matter anymore.

"Denise, I've given it a lot of thought and I want you to live with me. I don't want you out there in the streets living like a dog anymore. Besides, I'll be able to take care of you and I think you will be safe here." It didn't take long for me to move in; I didn't have much to move.

One day my mother and I were alone in the kitchen and she began to minister to me. "You got any idea what you're going to do with your life, Denise? You know you can't go on living the way you are living. You got Kim's grandmother trying to get you killed. It's time for you to make a decision. You got to lay them streets down. It's time out for all that. You gotta make some decisions about your future and about what you are going to do."

At this time, I was secretly sneaking around to see Kim, meeting at hotels to get high and fornicate. Sometimes I would go back to my mother's place so high that I didn't even go into the house. Instead, I would sleep on some tires in the garage until I sobered up. It felt different living with my mother this time because she really did care about me. While living with her, we were able to work on building a mother-daughter relationship, hash out some bad blood and ultimately come to love and accept one another, faults and all.

I remember one night in particular, we were sitting in the living room talking until the sun came up. "Denise, you know I was really messed up as a child. I couldn't be a mother to you because I didn't know how. I want you to

190

know that I always loved you. And sometimes when I stayed away it was because I was ashamed to come around. I didn't want you to see me all messed up the way I was. My head was out there in those streets, searching for love. Most of the time I didn't know what I was doing or who I was. I didn't know if I wanted to be a man or woman. I ended up having all y'all children and not taking care of any of you because I couldn't even take care of myself. I was drunk most of the time, passed out at the front door, trying to ease my own pain." Mother's voice began to shake. It touched my heart to see tears forming in her eyes. Oh, how she had changed! "I sincerely apologize for my wrong doings against you," she continued. "I want you to know I love you; I always have. Actually, I depended on you to take care of the little ones when I was out there in my addiction. I knew you were strong -- stronger than I could ever be. I knew you would take care of the little ones and hold things together. I saw you, trying to be a mother and a father to your brothers and sisters when you were nothing but a child yourself. I blame myself for the condition that your life is in because I wasn't there for you."

To my surprise, tears came to my eyes as well. I had never heard my mother share her feelings, and I never saw

191

her cry like this. I don't remember who reached out first, but we embraced. I accepted her apology, although she still had not taken full responsibility for the neglect and abuse that had damaged me emotionally. Mother was still growing in her relationship with the Lord and it was not until years later that she would fully understand the severe impact her actions had upon me, but this was a start.

*   *   *

Mother continued to invite different sisters to visit, hoping that I would bond with some of them. Whenever they showed up, I tried to avoid them. One day I was in my room lying down when I heard my mother calling me from the kitchen.

"Denise, I got someone I want you to meet, one of the sisters from church. Her name is Sister Jean Marzette." I didn't answer, but I was glad she gave me an advance warning because I began planning my escape right there on the spot. "Denise! Did you hear me? I said one of the sisters will be coming over later, and I want you to meet her."

"Yeah, I heard you," I finally hollered back. "Why you keep bringing them folks around here brothering me? I already told you I don't want anything to do with them ladies from church." Quickly I got up, got my clothes on and slipped out of the house when she wasn't paying attention. I headed up to the north side and spent the day shooting dope, playing pool and hugging up with one of my females. Because my mother's guests normally left around 9:00 p.m., I made sure I strolled in around midnight. When I opened the front door, I was surprised to see her guest still sitting in the living room. *Man,* I thought to myself. *You mean I still got to deal with this mess?* Without speaking, I marched past my mother's guest and straight to my room and closed the door. My mother was doing something in the back of the house, but she heard the door when I came in and made her way to the living room. "Denise, did you meet my guest?" she yelled from across the hall. As usual, I didn't answer. I was in my room, firing up some more drugs. When I didn't answer, she went to the living room by her guest. "Sister Marzette, did you meet my daughter?"

"No, she hasn't arrived yet. But I think one of your sons just came into the house, and he doesn't look good. He was pimping when he walked in, but he was staggering at the same time. I've never seen a walk like that before. I started to call you but I was afraid to move."

By this time, I had enough of all the mistaken identity and emerged from my room. I swaggered over to the recliner, still bent over and holding my crotch, and put my foot on the footrest to make the recliner sit upright and irritate my mother's guest. My mother didn't move, she just looked at me...hard.

"Hello sir," my mother's guest said, in a very pleasant tone. "My name is Sister Jean Marzette. It's a pleasure to meet you. You must be one of Sister Annie's sons." I cracked up laughing and, in a deep voice, introduced myself as DJ. I could tell she was checking me out, so I backed up and struck a pose so she could get a glimpse of all this man. Starting with my short afro, bandanna and baseball cap, slowly her eyes moved down to my short-sleeved dress shirt, then my blue jeans and finally, my high top gym shoes. I looked over at my mother and knew she was upset. On top of being as high as a kite, I was greasy and smelled like I had been wallowing in squalor all day.

"Who is this?" I said.

"Denise, why do you always have to act a fool? Didn't you just hear the sister introduce herself? Sister Marzette, this is my daughter Denise, the one I told you about." Sister Marzette just looked at me and smiled.

"I'm tired of meeting your people. I don't know why I always have to go through this with you. I didn't move in here for all this. This stuff is getting on my nerves." Although I was resistant, I could see God was using Mother and her God-given sisters to draw me out of the street. God was giving my mother a second chance to do right by me. Deep down I was touched by her effort, and I was proud of her.

When Sister Marzette and I locked eyes, she said "Lord Jesus, what in the world is this? Her whole life is messed up. Oh my God!" I was shocked to hear her stand up to me. Too shocked to reply, I let it ride. After that first encounter, Sister Marzette and I became good friends.

One Friday evening in May of 1986, I went to service and Elder Julius Wesley Collins happened to be preaching. He spoke with authority and control as he looked around the room, extending God's Arm of Salvation to the lost souls. My knees began to shake and I started fidgeting in my seat. A force greater than myself was troubling me. I sat there trying to pretend this steel-faced, lion-hearted preacher wasn't getting to me, but his stern look unhinged me. Suddenly I was no longer DJ; I was simply Denise. I felt like an old hollow tree, empty inside.

As the preacher concluded his message, he asked, "Will there be one tonight who would like to give their life to the Lord?" I straightened my slouch as he continued, "You may have gone out on God and kicked up your heels, but now it's time to pay your vow. Would you like to be saved?" Then emphatically he cried, "Fornicator! Where are you going to run? Where are you going to hide? There is no hiding place except in God. Don't just sit there in your seat. Come on, tell God yes!"

Behind him on the podium, I could hear the singers softly singing *"Come to Jesus; come while you have time..."* The preacher continued to prowl the room until he fixed his prophetic eye on me. Once again, I remained in my seat, stubbornly resisting the Voice of God. A part of me wanted to get up; I wanted to run to the altar, throw up my hands and surrender my life to God. But I didn't want to do it because I was afraid of dying, and that was all it would have been. I wanted to *want* to be saved; I wanted to ask God sincerely to change my life, and I wanted to mean it. But after so many years and so many chances, I doubted that day would ever come.

Then on Sunday, July 6, 1986, that day finally came. There was an altar call, and several visitors went up to the altar to receive prayer for salvation. As usual, I was still sitting in my seat, observing all that was going on around me, when the Holy Ghost led Elder Mosley to zero in on me. "Denise! What are you waiting for? God sent you here to be delivered from your sinful lifestyle. When are you finally going to allow God to do something for you?" When I didn't move, Elder Mosley continued sternly, "Don't continue sitting there, get on your feet before it's too late! Those streets are going to kill you! You've been coming here long enough to know this is what you need. Now come on, girl, before you die out there." He paused briefly, instructed the saints to pray that I would yield to the Spirit of God, and then continued. "You know God sent you here to be saved and delivered because you have a ministry. Don't die out of the Will of God." Softly, I began to cry.

Elder Mosley was addressing me in a stern tone because he was concerned about my soul, but the devil made me think he was yelling at me and trying to front me off. I didn't want to hear anything about dying. DJ was alive and well, and did not appreciate being yelled at. I felt embarrassed and was outwardly putting up a good front, although deep down I really wanted someone to come and walk with me to the altar. I didn't have the strength to stand up and make the first step on my own. So instead, I tilted my head, stared Elder Mosley right in his face…and did not flinch.

With his eyes fixed on me, Elder Mosley turned and walked away from the pulpit, down the stairs and straight toward me. Tiny beads of sweat erupted upon my forehead. I clenched my fists tightly as he came over to the edge of the pew where I was sitting and whispered in my ear, "Denise." I felt my fists loosen slightly; my heart was softening and my index finger began to twitch. "Denise," he whispered again, lightly placing his hand upon my shoulder. "What are you going to do, Denise? You know things are not going to work out in your life until you tell God yes. I know He's been dealing with you, so why don't you come on." His hand was still resting gently upon my shoulder. His entire demeanor had changed. Upon the podium, he was a warrior, but standing next to me, he was a compassionate, caring shepherd. My throat began vibrating and my mouth watered. I swallowed hard and tried to keep my lips together, but they fell apart. I shut my eyes and squeezed them as tightly as I could to keep the tears from falling, but tears gushed out through my eyelids as if I had an internal sprinkler system. They kept flowing, but I sat there hard like cement and began looking for an exit ramp. This gentle man was melting me down, treating me with care and compassion. No man had ever done that before. I didn't understand what was happening. I could feel myself softening, like butter left out overnight. I wanted to reach up and put my hand on his hand. I wanted to lay my face on it and weep. Finally, he reached down, gently took my hand and led me to the altar.

As I stood face to face with the deliverance warriors, I crumbled inside. My life was an open book before them all. I felt naked, wretched and undone. Tears flowed steadily from my eyes, soaking the shirt I was wearing as I thought of the abuse I had endured since childhood. I thought of the times I stared death in the face, and situations when acquaintances discovered me in semi-comatose states, with dope needles hanging out of my arms and breast. The times I lived on the run, dodging bullets, gang bangers, hit men, police officers, bats and chains. The times I slept in alleys, abandoned buildings, and the nights I didn't sleep at all. I thought about my childhood dreams, the nightmares that replaced them. The loneliness I endured, the gripping fears and the faces of those whom I tortured, it all grabbed me as I wailed and lamented on the altar. I couldn't continue to live that way. The madness had to end.

I was crippled before God. I cried out, "Jesus, help me! I'm so sorry. Forgive me, Lord. Oh, I'm so terribly sorry God. Forgive me for all the sin I've done. Please, Jesus, help me. Oh, God, I'm hurting so bad. Help me, Jesus." Everyone there could hear, see and feel my pain.

God allowed Sister Roshell to work with me on the altar that day. She asked if I was serious about giving my life to God *this time*. I shook my head yes, as the tears flowed down my cheeks. By the authority in the Name of Jesus and power of the Holy Ghost, the fearless deliverance minister laid her hand firmly on my forehead and asked God to destroy the yoke of sin that had me bound. She took dominion over the demons that controlled me and began to call them out with a loud voice. "Spirit of fornication, come out in Jesus' name!" Other demons were called out in like manner, but the spirit of lesbianism was very stubborn and didn't want to leave. As the Evangelist continued to call the demon out, it snarled savagely through me and said, "I will not come out!" My gruesome possessor churned wildly inside me and I began to gag and spit up blood. Nonetheless, this atrocious beast reluctantly bowed to the great and awesome Name of Jesus Christ. The demon of lesbianism packed its notorious bags and DJ moved out.

At once, I felt a calm come over me and I staggered about in amazement. I did not know that demons were real, or that they possessed me. I was totally dumb-founded, but I was finally free! A hearty praise filled the building that day as I praised and worshipped God with all of my might. I was electrified and ecstatic. My soul was free. "Thank you, Jesus," I repeated over and over. And the saints of God didn't mind praising Him with me either. I could hear their voices in the background shouting, "Praise Him, Denise! Praise Him!" The Good Spirit of God had gotten a hold of me and wouldn't let me go. The hand clapping, foot stomping and tambourine beating went on for a good while as the saints laughed, sang and danced with such joy. Even the children were pulled into the celebration. Many of them shouted and danced just as fervently as the adults did. Of course, I can't leave out the love of my life, my dear mother, whose tears flowed uncontrollably at seeing her baby set free by the Power of God. What a glorious time!

13

DEATH TO THE OLD MAN

It had been six months since I had gotten saved and I was convinced I couldn't live that life forever. My old lifestyle was calling my name and I found myself struggling with lying and manipulation. The sisters were looking sweet and juicy and I had a strong urge to just reach out and bite a couple of them! My stinking thinking was at work and I was contemplating leaving God.

I knew God was real, because He had changed me; fornication and drugs had ruled me for years, but were now mere testimonies of my past. Satan didn't tempt me with those things; mostly he toyed with my mind and my emotions. Low self-esteem and insecurity were becoming my dearest companions. In the streets, I learned to be aggressive, controlling and manipulative. Maybe I couldn't read books, but I could read people and situations. A certificate or diploma didn't mean anything; all I needed was a tough exterior and a lot of hype, and I possessed them both. Now I'll admit, I hadn't totally let lying and manipulating go. Not because I didn't want to be saved, I was simply afraid to trust God with my whole heart. I felt safer when I was in control.

So I continued to struggle with self, or more specifically sanctification. The core of sanctification is allowing one's self to be set aside for God's use. In order for that to happen, the true believer must be delivered from outward sins (such as fornication, stealing, using drugs, profanity, etc.), as well as inward transgressions (such as deceit, manipulation, hatred, and unforgiveness). The outward portion of sanctification seemed achievable; that was God's business. When I repented on the altar and asked Jesus to come into my heart, God removed the desire for drugs and fornication. However, the inside work was my responsibility, and I kept getting in the way. In order to be successful in my walk with God, I could not deviate from His Will for my life. I knew the Will of God was *my* sanctification. (I Thessalonians 4:7) That meant sanctification from DJ entirely; not only the outward behaviors (like the dip in my walk, the masculine clothing and the Fruit of the Loom underwear), but the *spirit* of DJ (the hustling, manipulating, hard-core stud). Sanctification seemed too great a mountain to climb. If I let DJ go, what would I have left? The concept of being open and trusting others didn't jive with me. To give up drugs and other vices was a relief, but my smooth rap and satiny dialogue were my survival tools. To exchange them for a life of righteousness made me nervous. It reminded me of the lesson I heard Elder Mosley teach about Adam and Eve scrambling through the bushes in the Garden of Eden, groping for fig leaves to veil their naked bodies. It wasn't so much their bodies they wanted to conceal, but it was their deep guilt and shame.

I felt I had too much going on within. I couldn't possibly tell the saints that my underlying agenda was to control and manipulate them because that was the only mode of survival I knew. I surely couldn't tell them that I've been thinking about leaving God! So I just sat there, bound.

The saints, however, were swift. The shrewd gift of discernment was quick in them. They used the Word of God to show me my foolishness and to build me up when they saw me striving to do right. The saints soon realized that I didn't see the big picture. I couldn't see that I was feeling awkward because this entire "God" thing was all so new to me. I just took it to mean that I didn't belong, that I didn't fit. My new thoroughfare on life was beginning to feel like a vigorous obstacle course, a course for which I had not trained or prepared. The Lord's plan to deliver me emotionally was being greatly held back by my own resistance. Often the saints of God uttered words of encouragement and exhortation to lift me up. Other times prophesy would spring forth and give me the strength to continue.

One morning, as I was preparing for Morning Prayer, the Spirit of God spoke to my heart and said, "Don't eat. Consecrate your spirit before me this day, for I will fill you with the Holy Ghost." I figured my imagination was playing tricks on me, so I ignored the Lord's Voice and satisfied my hunger with a bacon and egg sandwich and some orange juice.

During morning service, God moved greatly. The anointing of God fell like strong rain and many souls were baptized and filled with the Holy Ghost and spoke with other tongues as the Spirit of God gave them utterance, but I was not one of them. Embracing defeat and low self-esteem, my dearest companions, I left service sad and downtrodden because I disobeyed the Voice of God that morning.

The following morning, God beckoned ever so gently with the same instructions as the day before. As I was preparing for service, the Spirit of God spoke to my heart again and said, "Don't eat, but consecrate your spirit before me this day, for I will fill you with the Holy Ghost." I didn't intellectualize God's Voice this time. I quickly put the bacon and eggs away and closed the refrigerator door and high tailed it around the corner to be in service with the saints.

Faithful to His Word, the anointing stormed in on us. God used Presiding Elder Mosley to lay his hands on me and pray, and just as God promised, He filled me with the Holy Ghost,. We had what the old folks called *"chuch."* After that glorious day, my life began to radiate confidence and self-worth. The Holy Ghost booted out my former companion of low self-esteem and reigned in its stead.

God began to open doors for me to work in the field and share my testimony with souls who were bound in my former lifestyle. The evangelistic team visited substance abuse rehabilitation centers and nursing homes all across the Chicagoland area, and every time and opportunity was presented, I shared how God delivered me from the depths of street life. It was from these experiences that my ministry began to grow. Soon I was ministering to prostitutes, lesbians, homosexuals, dope fiends and homeless persons. Often I would go to the streets and bring hungry souls to *True Holiness Deliverance Ministry* on Sunday mornings to hear the Word of God.

As I continued giving myself to God through fasting, prayer and reading His Word, God began showing me portions of the ministry He had planned for me. I experienced vivid dreams through which the Lord's purpose for me was clearly revealed. God showed me that He spared my life all those countless times because He desired to raise me up to become a bold deliverance minister. He showed me that I was profitable to the ministry, that He had need of me and that He loved me.

Finally, God began speaking to me in dreams to convey His thoughts regarding my life. One night as I lay sleeping peacefully on my bed, the book of Samuel entered my dream and I was given instructions to read. When I awakened, I read how God called Samuel to be a prophet. The Word said God would call directly to Samuel at night, but because the prophet was not accustomed to hearing the Voice of God, he thought his master summoned him. Samuel went to his master repeatedly, but the puzzled man would tell him that he had not summoned him. After this happened three times, Samuel's master realized that it was the Voice of God the young lad had heard. He directed Samuel to reply "Yes, Lord" the next time he heard the voice. Samuel did as his master instructed and in return, Samuel became a mighty prophet before the Lord.

I became fearful after learning God wanted to use me as a deliverance preacher, and that fear became a great stumbling block to me. Old feelings of low self-esteem and inferiority began haunting me again. I fell into a slump and stopped seeking God with my whole heart.

Later that year, one of the saints told me about a position as a lunchroom attendant at the Chicago Board of Education. I applied for the job, was hired, and remained in my first legitimate position for two years. After two years, I applied for a position as a custodial assistant. It looked promising, but I had to meet with Miss Hernandez, a Board of Education official, to discuss my criminal background. A few days before the meeting, I attended morning service and the Spirit of God instructed the saints saying, "Don't ask God for anything this week, just thank Him." I followed those instructions to the T. All week long, I thanked and thanked and thanked Him. I thanked the Lord for His Goodness, His Mercy, His Forgiveness, His Compassion, His Provisions and so much more. When it was time for the meeting, I went to the Board of Education on the Southwest side of Chicago. Miss Hernandez asked me what I would do if I were in her position. I responded that the woman she was reading about in the black and white print of that file was not the same woman seated before her. I told her how God had changed my life and that I was no longer a criminal bound by forgery, theft, robbery or burglary. I told her how I had been justified and vindicated through Jesus Christ. I shared with Miss Hernandez my testimony that I was no longer a prisoner to the street life, but a prisoner of Christ. I am now bound only by my obligation to do that which is right in the eyesight of God and serve Him for the rest of my life.

Miss Hernandez listened attentively and after a brief pause, decided that I had the job (Hallelujah), but also informed me if any criminal activity occurred, I would be immediately terminated. Miss Hernandez stated that she did not know why she was giving me the job because it put her job on the line, but I understood God was using Miss Hernandez to bless me with employment.

God continued using Miss Hernandez as a blessing to me. After being on the job for six months, Miss Hernandez offered me a custodial worker position, and I began earning $800 every two weeks. Wow! I was so excited. Yes, I made thousands in the streets, but this was my first clean, honest living; a job that God had given me where I didn't have to worry about always looking over my shoulder. It felt good getting up every morning going to work, not having to scheme and plot, duck and dodge, watch my back and hope I didn't come up DOA.

Who Said It Couldn't Be Done?

I worked for the Board of Education from 1986 to 1993. In February of 1993, I became eligible for certification as a city employee with full benefits and pay. I found myself face-to-face once again with Miss Hernandez, only this time it was to discuss my termination. Because of my criminal background, I was denied eligibility for certification. There was nothing she could do; it was out of her hands. I was no longer employed with the Board of Education.

After my termination, my life seemed to nose-dive. I was flooded with negative emotions and mental anguish. I began questioning God. *Why did this happen after all these years? What do you want from me? What do I do now?*

My thoughts turned back to when I was in the streets making cash money. Tons of it rolled through my fingers, and I spent it as fast as it came. Here I was, living clean and sober and worrying about my future and contemplating whether I should return to my old lifestyle. I was concerned about paying my rent and making my car payment. I continued to think about why I lost my job – a job I know God provided. I could not see that God was still at work and that He wanted my full attention. During the years I worked for the Board of Education, I had become very relaxed and complacent, still fighting God's absolute purpose for my life. He had blessed me with the job, but I still had not sold completely out to Him in my spirit, and I was still refusing to do the job He called me to do: preach the Gospel. Instead of walking upright and humbling myself before God, I murmured and complained. I did not want to see or hear any talk about my so-called ministry. I didn't want anyone telling me how good God is or how God was molding me into a deliverance preacher through that situation. I did not want to hear how He was setting the stage for me to trust Him even in the bleakest of hours, when all hope seemed to be gone. To be honest, I didn't want to hear about God at all!

Further, I could not see how God was paving the way for me to continue my education and meet people of high social degree, and how He would use my life and testimony to preach Jesus to them all. I couldn't see how God wanted me to know Him as Father. Not just God, but God *the Father*, the tenderhearted Abba, my Daddy and Provider. I read in the Word how God said He would supply all of my needs according to His riches in glory by Christ Jesus. Despite my unbelief, God's Love and Kindness continued to sustain me. I was unemployed for approximately two years. During this period in my life, God did supply all my needs according to His Word. I did not see one hungry day or one homeless night. I did not go back out into the streets, but I still did not say yes to God's Will completely. I rebelled against God. I went to service and just sat. I did not clap my hands, stomp my feet or sing congregational praise songs. Sitting in those blue pews once again, the devil had me bound. Then one day in service, the preacher spoke; "The Lord giveth, and the Lord taketh away. Blessed be the name of the Lord!" That struck me sharply and I was done; done pouting, done occupying the pity pot, done moping and feeling sorry for myself. My eyes came open. God had allowed me to lose that job for a reason. During my unemployment, God demonstrated His keeping power and began bringing me to a place of total dependence upon Him. After that service, God began to deal with me and I allowed Him to soften my heart just enough to say yes to a small fraction of His Will: school. I enrolled in the General Equivalency Class at Olive-Harvey College.

At this particular time, I was living with one of the saints, Jakki, who supported me and encouraged me to press forward. The first night that I entered the classroom, it did not go well. Everything the teacher was talking about seemed so foreign. I felt out of place and incapable of learning anything. I was afraid to move in my seat, so I sat

212

still and looked straight ahead the entire class. When class was over I decreed never to return, but Jakki wasn't going for that.

"Now, Miss Jones, this is your first night. How are you going to quit just like that? What happened to all of the spunk DJ had, huh? You would fight a man twice your size and outrun savage dogs, but you can't sit in a classroom to receive your GED. No, I'm not buying it. You are going to class and you are going to finish. I believe in you, Miss Jones. Sure, it may be tough right now but you will get used to it. Just don't quit. You will never know what you can do and what barriers you can overcome if you quit now. You are not a coward. Whatever you do, just don't quit."

To ensure that I went, Jakki went to class with me every day and sat there the entire time until I completed the course. Sometimes when class dismissed she would teach me basic math: addition, subtraction, multiplication and division. I attended school four nights out of the week, and sometimes Jakki, who is a registered nurse, would come to class with me before working the night shift.

All I could see was the Love of God all around me. I remember scratching my head sometimes trying to figure out what kind of people these saints were. They did things

213

for me that no one had ever done before. They went to great lengths (at least I felt as if it was great lengths, but I later realized it's just what they do) to help me find my way in God and in life. They possessed the Love of God and allowed it to manifest in their lives through demonstration. Many times, I was brought to tears by some of the kind acts of love the saints bestowed upon me.

I became confident in school and after attending class for three weeks, I approached my teacher and told her that I was ready to take my GED test. My teacher did not share my confidence and expressed extreme concern. Nevertheless, I described my goal of becoming a substance abuse counselor and probation officer. I was ready to get on with my life and refused to be in a class for months. So the date was set for early one Saturday morning. Jakki and I drove to the testing site at Olive-Harvey College. We prayed before arriving, and again she encouraged me. "Miss Jones, you can do it! You can do it, Miss Jones!" I entered Olive-Harvey College to take my test. Although some of the questions still looked foreign to me, the Spirit of God directed me which answers to mark. When I finished my exam, I immediately began to doubt that I would receive my GED.

I had to wait four long and excruciating weeks before receiving the results but finally, the day came when the envelope arrived in the mail. Nervously I opened it. I PASSED! I was so excited that I jumped up and down and hollered loud enough for the entire block to hear me. I couldn't stop thanking and praising God. Tears flowed for a long time, only this time they were tears of joy. I was laughing and crying all at the same time. I could not believe it! I successfully completed the exam with a score of 247. Then I took the Constitution test and passed that! Oh! I was so happy. Thank you Lord! My life was beginning to turn around.

Some time after I had completed both tests, one of my teachers accompanied me to the office of Miss Vivian Thompson. Nervously, I sat in Ms. Thompson's office and wondered why she wanted to see me. "So Denise, here we are again," Ms. Thompson began. "Congratulations on your GED and constitution tests. I called you down here because I wanted to congratulate you personally and let you know how proud I am of you. Your story is one of the most remarkable stories I have ever heard. Denise, we want you to be the student speaker at your graduation ceremony. I, along with your teachers and some of the other administrators, all had a say in it and if you are willing, we would be honored to have you represent our school and your fellow classmates on graduation evening."

I was speechless. All I could do was smile. My life was spinning again, but in a most extraordinarily good way. Things were happening so fast I couldn't keep up with all of the blessings. They were coming back to back. What a remarkable honor and surge to my growing self-esteem! I could feel gratitude swelling in my heart as large as the Goodyear blimp. Who but God could change a life once destined to doom?

When I returned home, I told Jakki what Ms. Thompson said and we laughed and had a good time. The spirit of rejoicing was in the air and it would not let up. We went downtown to the Italian ice spot and celebrated with some slushies. It was beautiful to me. It wasn't long ago that I would have celebrated with some dope and a sleazy woman. It felt good having clean friends in my life and not having to chase a high. Instead, blessings were chasing me and knocking me off my feet. This was better than *any* high I had ever had!

Graduation night would soon become one of my greatest and most memorable events. It marked the joyous beginning of a trend of future accomplishments in a life once dominated by ill fate and loads of painful misfortune.

To join in the celebration and share my happiness, I shared my accomplishment with two of the ministers from my church: my spiritual father, Presiding Elder Donald L. Mosley and Elder Julius Wesley Collins.

"Elder Mosley, guess what!" I said with so much excitement. Before he could reply I blurted out, "I GOT MY GED!" There it went again, that mile-wide smile. "I did it, Elder Mosley. I passed with flying colors." Before he could respond, I blurted out again, "Guess who they want to give the class speech? ME! Elder Mosley, they asked me to do it!" I was so excited! I still had not come down from the high. I was out there, feeling good, enjoying life and having a good time.

All Elder Mosley said was, "Mmm, mmm, mmm." That's all it took for the smile to reappear; before long, Elder Mosley was smiling too. We looked like father and daughter, starring at one another and smiling the proudest smiles a father and daughter can smile. Elder Collins was right there with us, smiling too. Naturally, I invited them to attend the ceremony but was saddened to learn that Elder Mosley had already made plans for that day. I loved Elder Mosley just like a father. Since the time I became part of his ministry he had been extending himself to me, many times in the form of a rebuke, but his love would always shine through. I held fast to a few threads of hope. This man – his ministry, his caring way – had helped to change my life. He just had to be there!

I left and cried on Jakki's shoulder. "Oh, Jakki, I wanted him to be there. It's not going to be the same without him there…"

"Miss Jones, you will be okay. If he can't make it, you still must be strong. Hold your head up and represent your class with dignity."

The night of graduation, I frantically asked whether Elder Mosley was there. No one had seen him and I felt as if all the gloom in the world was overshadowing me. After all of the things I came through with Elder Mosley's help, through the ministry God gave him, he just had to be there.

While soaking in self-pity and defeat, Jakki suddenly said, "Denise, look: your father is here; Elder Mosley is here." I jumped up and caught a glimpse of him as he turned the corner, walking toward the auditorium. With him was Elder Collins. I could not believe it; they both had made it! What a moment!

As our eyes met, that silly grin slid clean across my face. I could tell, he was genuinely proud of me, the way a father prides in his daughter. I got out of line and ran to them. I restrained my tears and hugged my precious father. This man blew my mind. Oh, how my life had changed!

"Denise, look at you," he said. "You look beautiful tonight; so very elegant. I can't tell you just how proud I am of you."

Elder Collins also gave me a big hug. Everything was falling into place. I threw my head back proudly and marched to my seat with the rest of my graduating class.

Once the ceremony began, it wasn't long before I was called to the stage. As I walked nervously, I could feel butterflies tumbling in my stomach. I managed to make it up the stairs and onto the stage without stumbling. Once behind the lectern, I placed both my hands flat on the mantel and exhaled. Without thinking, I blew directly into the microphone. Before I began speaking, I took a moment to look around the room; I wanted to find my father. He was easy to spot; the brightest star in the balcony, center chair. Every nervous twitch seemed to cease the minute I laid my eyes on him, and I was able to sail through my speech.

Good evening, distinguished guests and friends. Welcome to our annual non-traditional graduation and recognition ceremony, class of 1993. Tonight is a special night for me. As I was sitting in my seat, I thought to myself that this gathering tonight could have been my funeral service, and let me tell you a little about why. Coming up the oldest of seven children in one of the roughest areas of Chicago, I was exposed to many things, mostly things that were negative. Coming from a broken home where my mother and father were drug addicts, I found myself as a child raising my younger brothers and sisters. Then, at the tender age of twelve years old, I was introduced to the street life. In case some of you don't know what the street life is, it is a life of drugs, crime, sex and a life of taking whatever you want and need to survive. I started using drugs at 12 years old. I began to hustle for money to feed my siblings. I would rob stores and stick up people as a teenager. I was incarcerated for one-third of my life. No! I'm not proud of that, but it happened. I went to school only because I had to, not because I wanted to accomplish anything in life. By the time I was in eighth grade, I lost all interest in school and only went to see who I could con out of something. When I passed to the ninth grade, I dropped out completely. I remember being so high from drugs that I jumped through a plate glass window and was pronounced dead on arrival at Cook County Hospital. However, the Lord gave me another chance. When I woke up, I woke up with 183 stitches. See, tonight could have been my funeral service. Several years ago, I was searching for a way out of that horrible lifestyle. I watched many of my close friends killed because of the street life that we were living. I went searching for a way out and something happened: I accepted the Lord into my life. He changed me. He gave me a reason to live. He gave me direction. He altered the very course of my life. From that point, I started working for the Board of Education and I held that job for seven years. I began to think as I was mopping floors, pulling garbage and cleaning windows for a living....Yes, it's a job and I was good at it, but I felt I had something I could offer others. I never had a mind to go back to school, but God gave me a mind to go back to school and here I am tonight, receiving my GED. To me, GED stands for Given Extra Determination, because that is what happened to me. Not only am I receiving my GED, but also I am going on to college to become a drug abuse counselor and probation officer. So tonight, I am proud of my accomplishment and I have much appreciation for God. Some of you here tonight might have great ideas about getting ahead in life. You might even get rich someday. I am here to tell you today that education is the basis for everything that you will ever encounter in life. Without education, self-knowledge has no meaning. Without education, how can you teach your children small things they must know for their foundation? Without education, how will you cope in this information-age of computer tech expressions? Education is one of the keys to giving a gift capable of enhancing your natural abilities, a gift capable of growing and growing and growing. In my closing, I would like to encourage somebody who might be listening tonight and might be involved in the same lifestyle that I was, to come on! You can make it! Go back to school and be whatever you want to be. I'm a living testimony that it can be done! Thank you.

I received a standing ovation. It took the audience a great while to calm themselves and be dignified again. Truly, God was glorified that night. When all of the commotion ceased and the audience managed to find their seats, Miss Carolyn Palmer, Director of Student Affairs, stepped up to the lectern, waving her hands on the sides of her face trying to cool herself. "Oooh wee, girlfriend," she said, "I can't touch that. All I can do is offer you a scholarship to continue to pursue your goals."

The audience went up again. Olive-Harvey College awarded me a four-year scholarship. Truly God was being magnified in my life. He was using me as a catalyst of hope for others. He brought me out so that He could bring others in. Me: a former dope fiend, a true menace to society, being used by THE ALMIGHTY God!

*   *   *

A few weeks later, I was beginning to come down from that high and reality was beginning to kick in. I still had to address God's plan for my life. I still had not given Him a total 'yes' to the way He endeavored to take me. I continued to fight and rebel against His Will regarding preaching and teaching His Word. Although receiving my GED and being the class representative were beautiful and unimaginable experiences, the truth of the matter is I wasn't so beautiful. I was content with God as long as He was blessing me, but when it came down to allowing Him to mold and make me, I fought Him tooth and nail.

The weeks turned into months and I continued to rebel. I would not receive instructions from the people of God. My behavior had become irrational. I didn't trust anyone anymore. I now guarded myself against the very saints of God who had nurtured me and given me hope.

When God dealt with the saints to back up from me, I became angry. They wanted to give God space to deal with me Himself, because they saw that He was endeavoring to teach me total dependence on Him; He was my Savior, but now He wanted to also become my Lord.

223

However, I didn't want God to deal with me; I wanted my spiritual father to deal with me. I could not bear the thought of Elder Mosley being upset with me. He was the first male I ever trusted. My self-worth revolved around his opinion of me. If he was upset or disappointed in me, I could not function. I didn't like the thought of him backing away from me. I felt rejected.

Had I received The Word of God through Elder Mosley's ministry, my emotional scars would have healed and I would have been more spiritually developed than I was. Nevertheless, my rebelliousness had me stuck in an emotional rut, and the only survival tools I possessed were those I learned in the street. That act of rebellion caused my entire life to spin completely out of control. I was acting as if God had not done anything for me. I was in this rage simply because I did not want to do God's Will and accept the route in life He destined for me to take.

A few years later on May 3, 1995, between the hours of four and five o'clock a.m., the Spirit of God visited me in a powerful vision as I lay upon my sleeping cot. I can't truthfully say whether I was asleep or awake, but I know the vision was from JEHOVAH God.

In the vision, I was in *True Holiness Deliverance Ministry* sitting by the window. A sister named Michelle, along with a few children – Talitha, Clara, and Ebony, and some other youngsters – were sitting with me. Presiding Elder Mosley was in the pulpit. I could see two mountains, one on the left side of the building and one on the right, and the center aisle was a bed of water. Just then, the children began walking and, very disturbed, Elder Mosley called out, "Where are they going?" Michelle began instructing Talitha to inform Elder Mosley about what was going on, but instead Michelle went to him herself. When she returned, she looked at me and said, "Come on, Denise, let's go across to the good mountain." I said, "No, no, no! I am tired. I am not prospering anyway, so you go ahead; I ain't going." Michelle continued to press me until I finally agreed to go. When I got in the water to proceed, I realized that I could not swim. Suddenly I found myself in the water with my mother and another member of my congregation, Sister Wendy. I took hold of my mother and asked Wendy to take hold of me. My mother pulled us across to the good mountain and climbed up until I could not see her anymore. I turned to Wendy and said, "I'll go up first, then pull you up." Wendy was too short to climb alone.

As I climbed up the mountain, I passed words like Fornication, Masturbation, Adultery and Oral Sex. These words were engraved in the mountain. When I got closer to the top, Sister Wendy's daughter Clara, was standing on the top of the mountain pointing and saying, "Auntie Denise, that says Lesbianism." I agreed and continued to climb. Finally, I reached the top of the mountain and Wendy was standing there pointing to the final word. "Doesn't that say Lasciviousness? Do you know anything about that?" I said, "Yes, I used to be like that." One thing I noticed was that all the words were engraved and carved in the mountain except the words Lesbianism and Lasciviousness, those were large protrusions sticking out of the mountain like stony ledges, wide and thick.

Then the Spirit of God commanded, "Don't look back!" but I wanted to see how far I had climbed, so despite God's warning, I looked back and immediately found myself standing on the evil mountain, engulfed in flames. Terrified, I cried out repeatedly with all of my might "Jesus, Jesus, Jesus!"

Just then, a great light shining brilliantly reached down from above, pulled me out of the midst of the flames, and placed me back on the good mountain. I was down on the ground balled up in a knot, but looking up at the light. The light was in the form of a hand. It was shaking its finger and pointing at me. Out of the midst of the light I heard a great voice commanding, *"Be still. Don't move. Be still. Don't move."*

Just then, I awakened; dripping with sweat, my heart pounding, and sitting bolt upright in the bed. The vision was over and I was horrified. This was a fear more gripping than death, more frightening than facing my enemies, more notorious than the rapists that sent me crashing through a thick, pane-glass window. This was serious.

God dealt with me and opened my understanding to the vision. My sitting on the pew by the window represented my position in God. I had become distracted and preoccupied with the world. Selfishly I thought only about the things I wanted and how I wanted my life to go. My growth was at a standstill. I was not on fire for God. I was just sitting there taking up space, that's all. I became a hindrance and a stumbling block.

The mountains represented choices I had to make. They had a lot to do with the war and struggle within me. I was in the seat of indecision but now God was requiring that I make up my mind. I must choose between the world and sanctification. I thought about the scripture that says, *For the good that I would, I do not. . . when I would do good, evil is present with me* (Romans 7:19-21), and another which asks the question, *How long halt ye between two opinions?* (I Kings 18:21), and yet another which states, *Choose ye this day whom ye will serve* (Joshua 24:15). I should have made up my mind years before to go all the way with God, but I hadn't.

Elder Mosley's position in the pulpit represented leadership. I should have been giving the most earnest heed to every word he spoke and obeyed his instructions, but I didn't. I wasn't paying attention. I was too busy just looking out the window.

Michelle represented help. Sometimes God would plant a saint right in my path to exhort or encourage me. He was extending His Grace and Mercy, but I was refusing it. All I had to do was cry out to God and He would have delivered me out of all my troubles, but rebellion had me bound.

The children represented all the souls whom God allowed me to witness to and bring to our services. When the children got up and began walking, Elder Mosley spoke sharply and said, "Where are they going?" God was angry with me. I had become a hindrance and a stumbling block to the souls who were mere babes in the Gospel. God could have moved me out of the way at that very moment, but He didn't. Instead, He sent help by way of Michelle saying,

"Come on, Denise, let's go across to the good mountain."
Yet I continued to resist. Bound to my seat and convinced
by the devil that I just could not make it, I exclaimed, "No,
no, no! I am tired. I am not prospering anyway, so you go
ahead; I ain't going." This showed my defeated state of
mind. Although God had delivered me from drugs and
lesbianism, I still was unable to see myself as anything
more than a failure. Though I had obtained my GED, I still
saw myself as a fourth grade drop-out. Because of
stubbornness and rebellion, I had not allowed God to heal
me and bring me to the place where I could see Christ in
me. Because of this, I was unable to understand how God
could use me to preach His Word to others; I couldn't see
how He could use me for anything at all.

The water in the center aisle between the two
mountains represented the Word of God. If I had only
received the Word, it would have cleansed me thoroughly.
Again, the scripture rings over in my mind, *That He might
sanctify and cleanse it with the washing of water by the
word* (Ephesians 5:26). God was showing me that I must
allow His Word to saturate my spirit so that I may be clean
and have sweet fellowship with Him and His Son in the
Holy Ghost. My soul was thirsting and longing for that, but

my flesh – the natural, unregenerate side of me – continued to fight.

When I finally submitted and got in the water, I did so grudgingly. It wasn't that I wanted to please God with all my heart, I just knew that if I was going to have any kind of peace, I had to obey God.

While crossing over I realized I could not swim. God was showing me that although I thought I knew it all, I really did not know a thing. He was proving that He was my source of strength. My help would come from Him. There are things in His Word that I cannot understand on my own, so I need His guidance and direction. The scripture says, *Howbeit when he, the Spirit of truth, is come, he will guide you into all truth* (John 16:13). In the dream, my mother represented just that. She gripped my hand, just as a mother does when crossing the street with her child, and led me to the mountain of sanctification. She was a mature saint, one who listens to the Spirit of God and walks according to His word. Wendy represented someone that would come to God after me and would have the same trouble I was presently having. I would be able to minister from the Word just as the mother figure did to me. After all my fighting and bucking, I still didn't realize that my freedom and deliverance depended on my obedience to the Word of God.

The words Fornication and Masturbation represented things I had to overcome, and the people I passed on the way up the mountain represented the souls God would allow me to help overcome those spirits.

Lesbianism and Lasciviousness protruded more than the others because they were my strongholds. I am easy prey to those snares unless I depend wholly on God, remain in His Will and allow Him to keep me.

My looking back represented my disobedience and rebellion against God. It represented my backsliding. Suddenly finding myself on the evil mountain engulfed in flames showed me that I would have trouble and turmoil should I turn back on God. There will be no peace in my life, only catastrophe, great affliction and misfortune. God will allow the devil to be loosed on me like a roaring fire. The force of demon powers will consume me. My life and well-being will be on the line. Similar to actual fire victims, I would have physical handicaps and emotional and mental scars that would never mend.

The glorious light that lifted me out of the flames, was Jesus Christ rescuing me once again from my sins. I called on Jesus truly from the depths of my soul and He delivered me. The irony of it all is that when He delivered me, He placed me right back on the mountain of sanctification, which is the only way of life prescribed by God for man to life. I thought about the scripture in Isaiah 35:8 that reads, *"And an highway shall be there, and a way, and it shall be called The way of holiness; the unclean shall not pass over it; but it shall be for those: the wayfaring men, though fools, shall not err therein."* Sanctification is a mountain, which every saint of God must climb. There is no getting around it. The Word of God says, "For this is the will of God, even your sanctification...." (I Thessalonians 4:3). As far as my ups and downs, the lesson I learned is a simple one: be still and don't move.

> *I've had many tears and sorrows, I've had*
> *questions for tomorrow. There were times*
> *I didn't know right from wrong. But in every*
> *situation, God gave blessed consolation that my*
> *trials come to make me strong. Through it all,*
> *through it all, I've learned to trust in JESUS, I've learned*
> *to trust in God. (Ohhh) Through it all, through it all, I've*
> *learned to depend upon His Word.*

I am grateful for this dream because it showed me the Grace and Mercy of God. Many times, I felt like it couldn't be done, but when I thought about it I had to ask myself, "Who Said It Couldn't Be Done?" The only answer I could come up with was ME. As I look back over my life, everyone who was significant in it always tried to help me and was hurt when I didn't succeed. Through all my difficulties, the lessons learned far outweigh the tests and trials themselves. I am stronger and wiser, more compassionate, empathetic and understanding of the needs of others. My life's circumstances have worked patience and endurance in me, but most of all, I have the assurance of knowing IT <u>CAN</u> BE DONE.

14

OUT OF THE BELLY OF THE WHALE

When the word of the Lord spoke unto Jonah to go and cry against Nineveh, Jonah went to Joppa and found a ship going to Tarshish to escape the presence of the Lord. The Lord sent out a great wind into the sea and there was a mighty tempest in the sea. The ship was in danger of being wrecked. Jonah eventually was cast into the sea, but the Lord had prepared a great fish to swallow up Jonah. After spending three days and three nights in the belly of the whale, the Lord spoke unto the fish, and it vomited out Jonah upon the dry land.

Like Jonah, I traveled many avenues trying to escape the presence of the Lord. My Tarshish was shooting heroin, smoking cocaine, dropping pills, drinking cough syrup, pimping and committing crime. I stayed in the belly of the whale for eight years.

On Sunday, July 6, 1986, I finally gave God my will, and what was left of my life. By this time, I was as Shug said in *The Color Purple*, "You sho' is ugly." And believe it: I was whipped. My face was so bumpy it looked like the Rocky Mountains. I had big, black spots the size of nickels and quarters all over my face. My teeth were literally so loose that I could have performed my own dental extractions. Whenever I touched them, blood flowed from my gums like a mountain stream. My body was in bad shape. When I moved my head, I felt my brain shifting; for years, I experienced terrible headaches. My hands and feet were swollen to the size of footballs. I could not get any shoes on and had to tie my feet down on top of my shoes with a rope, belt or anything that was strong enough to hold them in place. When you think of the creature from the Black Lagoon, that was the old DJ. Every time I looked in the mirror, I scared myself. Actually, ugly is an understatement.

Today, I can say I no longer hear voices, no longer shoot heroin or pop pills. I no longer rob and stick up, steal or carry guns or knives. I do not have sexual relationships with women. I no longer beat women and put them on the corner to sell their bodies. I don't play checks or credit cards, and I no longer steal other people's identities. I do not go toe-to-toe with men, neither do I wear men's clothing or tie my breasts down with Ace bandages, attempting to deny my femininity. I am comfortable with my gender and sexuality.

I traveled down many avenues before I finally allowed the Lord to place me upon dry land. After God showed me my state through a most powerful dream, I hit the ground running. In addition to my GED, I obtained a Bachelor of Arts in Applied Behavioral Sciences from National Louis University, then a Master of Science in Nonprofit Management, with a concentration in Human Service Administration from Spertus College. I am also a Certified Addictions and HIV Counselor and desire to open a sober living housing facility for women. *Tender Touch, Inc.* will provide services to women who are reentering society from prison and will offer GED classes, job-readiness skills training seminars and parenting classes. All of these skills are necessary to live socially productive and personally victorious lives.

God has anointed me to be a deliverance minister, allowing me to preach to women in various drug treatment facilities, jails, homeless shelters and on street corners from the northern streets of Chicago to the southern roads of Florida. Then, in 2005, God blessed me to minister during a Friday evening service at *True Holiness Deliverance Ministry.*

In sum, I have twenty-three years of sobriety. Who Said It Couldn't Be Done? I am living proof:

IT CAN BE DONE!

Therefore if any man be in Christ, he is a new creature: old things are passed away; behold, all things are become new.

II Corinthians 5:17

I can do all things through Christ, which strengtheneth me.

Philippians 4:13

Who Said It Couldn't Be Done?

THE WITNESS PROGRAM

*The following are testimonials of a few
of Denise's family members and friends who knew her back
in the day and witnessed her folly and madness…*

*   *   *

Who Said It Couldn't Be Done?

<u>Denise and her mother – Annie Mae Freeman</u>

Who Said It Couldn't Be Done?

I loved Denise, even back then when I was young and didn't know the first thing about love or being her mother. I always knew she was smart. When I was running wild in the streets, I knew she could hold things down. I felt bad about putting all my responsibilities on Denise. She was just a child. I was just too busy running the street, hustlin' and doing my thing. Soon Denise and I were out there together, but she passed me up. Denise started doing things that never entered my mind to do. I didn't think she would ever find her way out off the streets. A miracle happened; she did come out of the streets. When I look back on things and see how we all have changed, it's just a miracle... I know it's GOD because Denise to still be alive to tell her story. I am proud of you, Denise. I am proud and I love you.

Who Said It Couldn't Be Done?

<u>Stanley – Denise's Brother</u>

Denise is my oldest sister. At first, I thought she was cool, but then she started doing crazy things. She had become so scandalous; I would tell people that I didn't know Denise. She was straight bogus - doing things for no reason. The way she was back then, it didn't seem possible for her to change. It just seemed like she was who she was, and she would never change.

Now everything is lovely. A true change has taken place in her life. Denise is not the same person. I am not afraid to go to sleep around Denise. In the past, if you slept around her, it was nothing for you to wake up with your pockets cut off and your wallet missing. I am glad and happy for Denise. Someone would have killed her, if she had continued living that horrible lifestyle.

Benesse – Denise's Sister

As long as I can remember, there was something criminal about my sister. I was seven or eight years old, when I realized there was something seriously "not right" with her. I don't know how to put it, she was really really a bad person. When I was growing up, I saw all the trouble she was causing in the family and in the neighborhood. Denise was the star attraction in our family. Although she was a terror, I was fascinated with her. She was the person that caught my attention. I watched her every move.

Denise was different from all the other girls that I knew. She dressed like a boy and act like a boy, but she didn't want to have anything to do with boys. I can recall only one boy having a crush on her, but she did not like him; she liked his sister. It was at that time that I realized

Who Said It Couldn't Be Done?

Denise was into girls. I also noticed her criminal activities. Her life was exciting. I began to accept her and I wanted to be a part of the same lifestyle that she was living. However, when I got old enough to have my own place, I became fearful for Denise's life. She was living with me and her enemies would come to my house with guns and busting out my windows trying to get to her because of the things she had done; such as stealing, robbing and fighting. I know it's only the Grace of GOD that she is still alive. I remember the crazed, murderous look in some of their eyes.

Now that Denise's life has changed, she really is my role model. I still find her life exciting. I have the utmost respect for my sister. She is my role model. When she went back to school and graduated with her degrees, I can't express how proud I am of her accomplishments and reaching her goals. Now when I see my sister, she is no longer wearing men's clothing and Fruit of the Loom underwear. She wears lace and feminine attire. It really blesses me because I know that she has changed. There were times when I saw her in her past life and I knew she was miserable, especially when she was living her life as a man. She tried to put on a happy face when she was with her women, but whenever they were not around, her entire demeanor changed. She would soften up just a little and act a little more feminine. She acted more like my sister and not some hardcore dude; that was just the front that she had to wear. I learned a lot from my sister and she is truly my example. I truly love my sister and I just hope and pray that she continues doing the Will of God. I still hang with her, but this time for all the right reasons; ministering and sharing our testimonies of how God mend and put families back together. Denise, you are my inspiration and I love you so much.

George Jones – Denise's Brother

Back then, yeah, things were bad. Denise was getting high, stealing and lying, but she was bringing all of the goodies back home, so I was cool with it. We didn't have anything. She was providing and taking care of my needs. What was I going to say? Naw, I was cool, at least until she turned on me. When I was seventeen years old, Denise stole my car. All I could do was shake my head; my sister was a rogue – she was lowdown and dirty. I don't know why she was a terrible person.

I really hurt many days over our situation. I had already lost my Mother to the streets. To watch my sister take that same path was difficult; I was hurting. I was losing everyone who was important to me; I didn't understand why. Life was hard and unfair. I would hear people talking about Denise and how lowdown she was. I tried to block all of that out of my mind because it hurt and I did not want to lose another love one. I thought Denise was tough when she jumped through that glass window and almost died. I was in a lot of pain about that too. I'm glad to say that she is still here. I am so very proud of my sister. Denise has come a long way.

Angela – Denise's Baby Sister

Having Denise as a big sister is beautiful. I have someone to look up to. She has shared her past lifestyle with me. She has taught me the ways of the street and the things I should look out for in the streets. She encourages me to stay in school and go as far and as high as I can. She reminds me that every goal is obtainable as long as I stay with God. Yes, we have our difficulties, but I can count on her to be there for me no matter how many mistakes I make. I know she loves me for who I am. Therefore, if you ask me how I feel about having her for a sister, I will tell you that I would not trade her for anything because I really love my big sister.

Family Portrait

Back row (from left): Jermaine, Angela, Denise, Stanley.

Front row (from left): George, Annie Mae and Benesse.

(Absent: Regina)

Who Said It Couldn't Be Done?

San

DJ and I go way back. It was nothing nice. Although we were hommies, we could not trust each other because every man was looking out for himself. Because of our lifestyles, we were jam-tight, all we did was stick-up, get high, run games and make money. We had a lot of fun and did many stupid things. Today, when I look at Denise, I am very proud of her. Denise should have been dead a long time ago. When I see Denise today, I know it is GOD's doing... Denise, I still love you, Man.

<u>Moochie</u>

DJ was wild and crazy, but she was a lot of fun. Denise was just wild. She did things I wouldn't dare do, like when we were robbing people, she would pull out a blade and just cut the victim's pockets off. She was smooth with it too and she never made them bleed. Denise took too many chances. Everyone wanted to beat her. She was out there stealing and messing with other people's girlfriends back in the day. She was putting her life on the line, but that didn't seem to matter to Denise. She was a real thug. I would tell her all the time that life wasn't for her. Although I was out there, I always told Denise to go to school and get her life together, but she was hardheaded and didn't listen to nobody. Denise was something else back in the day. Now that Denise has changed, I count my blessings. I am glad that Denise and her mother are still in my life. I am glad that she has come out of the streets and the gay life. I'm glad that she is saved. Denise is constantly climbing the ladder; she is trying to reach the top. I am proud of her, not just for one thing, but for many things. All that Denise has been through; she is truly an inspiration to me. Her life should be a movie…

Who Said It Couldn't Be Done?

Dee

I met Denise when I was in third grade. I was a best friend to Denise's sister. Denise was scary looking. I had never seen a black female pimp before and her presence terrified me, but it also intrigued me. I wanted to know more about this image I saw on a daily basis. Denise was heavily into drugs and alcohol. She would stand over me at times and ask me if I was afraid of her. I was and she would calm me down by saying that she would not hurt me because I was a friend of her sister and she was going to look out for me. Denise and I bonded. She did look out for me. Most of the time Denise was laid back.

When I first met her she had two Caucasian girls on her side that she was pimping. Her sister told me those girls were her women. They were her girlfriends and she was their man. My mind was blown. To see a woman living her life as a man and laying with women was a bit much for a third-grader, but I had to keep coming around. I asked many questions. Her sister told me that was just the way Denise was and that it was normal for Denise to live her life as a man, so I accepted it. Denise was a cool man – just like a guy, all calm and collected. She played around and had fun, but most of the time she was just laid back, getting high and laying up with her women. She ended up being the coolest guy I ever met. Until she got strung out – then she was a terror…

When I first heard about Denise's conversion, I did not believe it. I was like, "No way…" but when I saw her for myself, it was unbelievable. She was dressed like a lady – wearing a dress. Man! That was weird! However, it was beautiful too. Denise had come from one drastic lifestyle into a new one. I rejoiced for her.

Denise, it was all for the glory of GOD and I am glad that He used you as that vessel to make an example for others. Your lifestyle was not in vain. Keep doing what you are doing. You are the vessel God is using to save and change lives in a great and mighty way. If GOD did it for you, I know there is hope for the universe…

Faye

I will never forget how I met Denise Jones; her presence that day changed my life's path. One day at work, in walks this energetic lady into my office inviting me to her graduation. I'm thinking to myself, *Who is this lady and why is she inviting me to her graduation?*

We had been working together for about three years but we never spoke to one another aside from a few good mornings and good nights. Stunned at her odd and unexpected request, I replied, "I won't be able to attend your graduation, but maybe I'll buy you a card..." She stated, "I don't want your money, I want your presence." It did not matter that I said, "No Repeatedly!" Denise would not take no for an answer.

Well, I did attend her graduation and on that day, she showed a brief time capsule of her rocky past to the present. I was totally impressed; the video left me sobbing in tears. I began to see Denise in a different light; I came to admire Denise's drive and approach in doing things the right way. Her views of how she analyzed things puzzled me, though; I remember thinking, why does she try so hard? I didn't understand then, but I clearly understand now.

After that, I was drawn to her like a magnet; it was her tenacity for life and her love for God. I would continue to ask her questions about God and because she proved so knowledgeable, I asked for her help understanding the Bible. Anyone that knows Denise knows that's the Word of God is her favorite topic. Our conversations became endless. I inquired how she made it so far because of her trials and tribulations were so many. Denise explained to me that she strives to keep God first in everything she does.

Denise's accomplishments are awesome. It wasn't long before we were the best of friends. I'm happy to say that it was through Denise witnessing to me, I got saved and I am learning what "True Holiness Deliverance" really means. I am so grateful that I went to her graduation because it changed my entire life.

Who Said It Couldn't Be Done?

Catrina

Denise was strange to me. She was wild as if she had come from the jungle. She did not seem human. She had no social graces *what so ever!* She was totally uncouth. She seemed incapable of adapting to civilization and living life as normal people lived. Rules and structure seemed foreign to her. I remember seeing Denise breaking into project apartments by climbing in through the windows, stealing whatever she could carry out. She also broke into our apartments through the window crushing my dollhouse and stealing our food stamps.

When I learned that The Lord had saved Denise, I followed her progress. I needed to know that she had been converted – for real… It has been a twenty-year journey that I have witnessed the miraculous Power of God working in Denise's life. She is a true miracle. I am proud of Denise.

Who Said It Couldn't Be Done?

Tina

I am so proud of Denise. She was out there in the street in a bad way. I never did like seeing her out there like that. I always told Denise to get her life together and go to school because the streets were not for her. Denise was always special. She always tried to help others, even when she was robbing and stealing. She came looking for me when I was in my addiction. To see Denise on the right track in her life gives even more hope to old-schoolers like me. I feel good about Denise making it out because she didn't belong out in the streets. I feel like I had something to do with it. Denise always told me that she looked at me as if I was her mother. I guess for a few years, I was her mother. Denise and I were close. We used to talk all the time and I always tried to steer her in the right direction – just like a mother. To see Denise on track makes me proud.

Who Said It Couldn't Be Done?

Maricela

When I meet people that say "I can't", I like to tell them about Miss Jones. She was a drug addict and a grade school dropout with an IQ that was significantly below average. When I met her over four years ago, she was in the process of completing her Bachelor's degree. Since then she has gone on to get her Master's degree and is currently enrolled in a Ph.D. program. I do not mean to say that these things came easily to Miss Jones as I have seen her struggle. It is her faith and perseverance in the face of difficulties that make her story one worth sharing.

Jean

When I met Denise, she was a hard core lesbian and drug addict. She dressed like a man, she walked like a man and she talked like a man. Her mother had invited me over to talk to her. At the time I saw her, I wanted to run. Denise looked hard and rough. I was afraid of her. When her mother introduces me to her, God gave me a desire to really reach for Denise and help her. As I begin to work with Denise, she still struggled with her drug addiction. One day I entered her room and Denise had overdosed on drugs, but God had mercy and spared her life. As God blessed me to continue to pray for Denise, she finally gave up her will. The Almighty and Awesome God, drew Denise by His Spirit with love and kindness.

Today, the beautiful, blossom flower that she has developed into brings joyful tears to my eyes. I know where she came from. As she continues to pursue her

Doctor's Degree in Organizational Leadership and open a Sober Living Housing for Women, she realizes that this only can be achieved through God. According to *II Corinthians 5:17...Therefore is any man be in Christ, he is a new creature: old things are passed away; behold, all things are become new.*

From out of The Hands of The Potter, God has craftily designed and molded this new creature, who is proclaiming His Great Gospel of True Deliverance. And with the help of God, her final destination will be to see Jehovah God, high above the clouds and His Beloved Son, Jesus Christ.

Who Said It Couldn't Be Done?

Jakki

Denise was a mess when I first met her. I didn't know her out in the streets. I met her after GOD saved her. But, boy oh boy, she was a piece of work. In the very beginning, I knew the role I played in Denise's life was to help her develop as a woman of GOD and as a woman in general. Denise had very little, if any, feminine qualities and characteristics. To look at her in a dress seemed abusive. She was harder than most men. There was nothing demure about her. But little by little, down through the years, I have watched GOD transform Denise from a man to woman. The transformation has been long and tedious, but beautiful. Denise has blossomed into a lady more beautiful than any of us had imagined. She has grown from a fourth grade education to a Master's Degree; from a man to a lady; from a menace to society to being a law-abiding citizen. Truly, The Lord is Magnified in Denise's life.

Shirley

I am a seamstress and one of my customers referred Denise to me thirteen years ago. When we spoke on the phone, she asked me to make her a white skirt. When we finally met, she was friendly but masculine. I really didn't know what to make of her, however we talked about the type of skirt she wanted. She wanted a skirt with no split and with side pockets. I just couldn't understand how she was going to walk without a kick pleat in the back of the skirt. We argued because I wanted to put a spilt in it. She refused, and told me to make what she asked for. I made her skirt and was glad to get rid of her. Denise being Denise, you don't get rid of her, she is persistent in whatever she wants. I became her seamstress and eventually her friend.

Who Said It Couldn't Be Done?

Denise would come to my house every week with all kinds of fabric; she would create and design clothing she wanted me to make, especially denim skirt suits. I would make two to three suits a week. She would have me up to the wee hours of the morning sewing. She would always say, "I want to look feminine," and as time went on, she did. She would have me make her feminine dress suits. She would wear my suits to church with matching shoes. I said, "Go on, girl. Where is your purse?" This girl would not carry a purse, even when she was all dressed up.

I must say we had some good talks, especially about her past. I was flabbergasted. I could not believe that a person could go through all the things she encountered in one lifetime and live to tell about it. She never had trouble witnessing about her life, her testimony, her salvation and mostly about her God. Denise uses every opportunity to talk about God in everything she does and everywhere she goes. She loved to talk about how her God saved her. She is never at a loss for words and is always helping others.

Her story and her life are a true testimony to how God can save and bring you out of any kind of abuse, drug addiction, prostitution and crime. She is truly a woman of God.

Denise Jones' Arrest Reports
1975 - 1986

Denise's crime spree lasted eleven years. It began at the age of fifteen for disorderly conduct, impeding the arrest of a friend. Her last act of violence occurred on February 20, 1986, just five months before she gave her life to Christ. Since that time, Denise has lived her life free from drugs and crime.

Who Said It Couldn't Be Done?

In 1975, Denise was arrested for disorderly conduct.
Her rap sheet is not available because she was a minor.

Arrested November 8, 1978

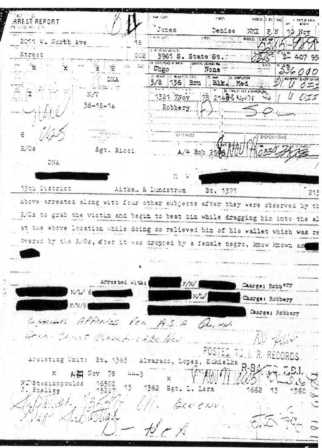

2011 West North Avenue
Assault and Robbery

**Observed by police officers beating and
robbing a victim in an alley.***

---

* See page 130.

Who Said It Couldn't Be Done?

Arrested December 28, 1979

500 Oak Street
Home Invasion and Robbery[*]

---

[*] See pages 134-135.

Arrested February 25, 1981

1501 North Ashland-Disorderly Conduct

**Arrested for impeding the investigation of
a theft causing a breach of the peace.**[*]

---

[*] See page 137.

Arrested March 16, 1981

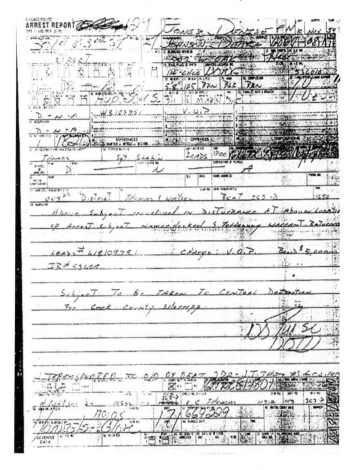

301 East 63rd Street – Disorderly Conduct

**Arrested for disorderly conduct and
an outstanding warrant for violation of probation.**[*]

---

[*] See page 146.

Who Said It Couldn't Be Done?

Arrested December 8, 1981
29th & Green-Auto Theft/Robbery
Arrested while driving a
vehicle reported stolen during a robbery.

Who Said It Couldn't Be Done?

Arrested August 16, 1983

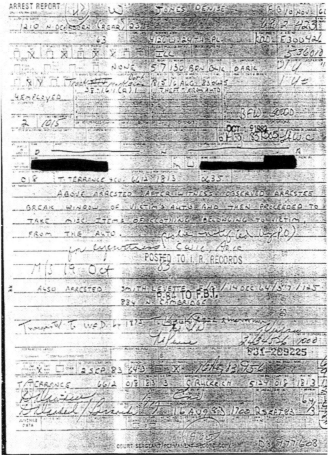

1210 North Dearborn - Robbery

Arrested for breaking and entering a vehicle and stealing miscellaneous items from the vehicle.

Who Said It Couldn't Be Done?

Arrested August 21, 1983

1010 North Rush Street-Prostitution

Arrested for soliciting an undercover officer to perform sexual intercourse for the sum of $50.00.

Who Said It Couldn't Be Done?

Arrested July 27, 1984

61 East Huron-Theft
Criminal Damage to Property

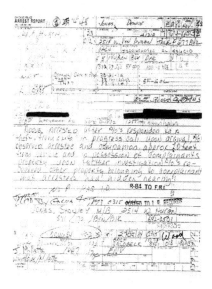

Who Said It Couldn't Be Done?

Arrested May 7, 1985

328 East 47th Street-Stolen Vehicle

Arrested for driving a stolen vehicle and
possession of numerous stolen credit cards.

Who Said It Couldn't Be Done?

Arrested July 29, 1985

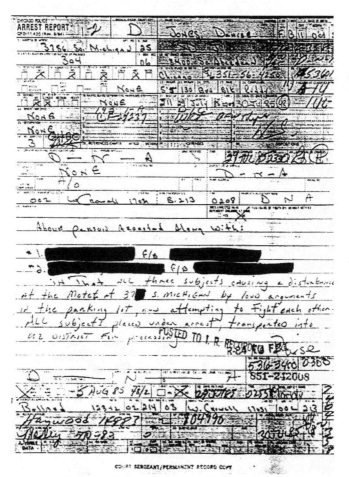

3756 S. Michigan-Disorderly Conduct

**Arrested for fighting in the motel parking
lot and using a stolen credit card.**

Who Said It Couldn't Be Done?

Arrested August 13, 1985

1154 S. Michigan-Theft

Arrested for attempting to leave the hotel without paying the bill.[*]

---

[*] See page 152.

Who Said It Couldn't Be Done?

Arrested February 20, 1986

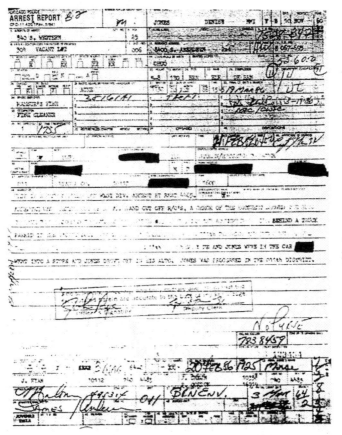

340 South Western-Theft

Arrested for breaking into trucks and stealing merchandise.

Who Said It Couldn't Be Done?

Denise's Mother: Annie Mae Jones

Photo Gallery

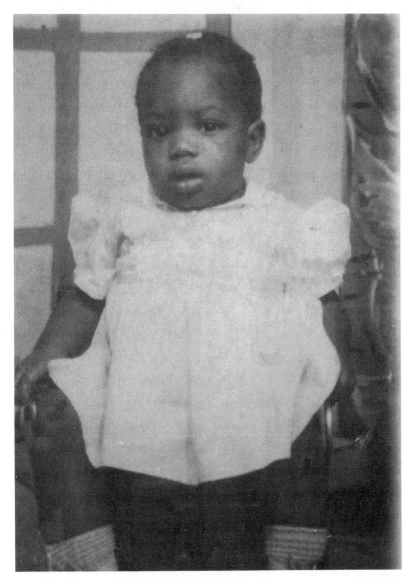

Baby Denise

Who Said It Couldn't Be Done?

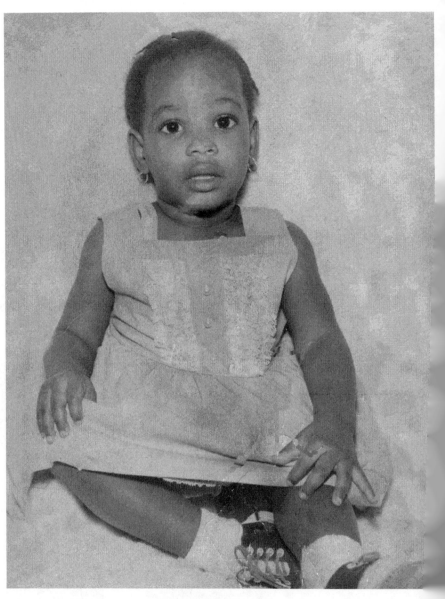

Baby Denise

Who Said It Couldn't Be Done?

DJ – 1976

Who Said It Couldn't Be Done?

1993 GED Graduate
Olive-Harvey College
Student Speaker

GED stands for Given Extra Determination,
because that is what happened to me.

Who Said It Couldn't Be Done?

2007

Graduated from National Lewis University
Chicago, Illinois
Bachelor of Arts in Applied Behavior

Who Said It Couldn't Be Done?

**2009
Graduated from Spertus College
Chicago, Illinois
Master of Science in Non Profit Management**

Denise's Aunt and Uncle

Who Said It Couldn't Be Done?

Denise's Grandmother

Who Said It Couldn't Be Done?

My message to the masses:

Who Said It Couldn't Be Done?

Everybody has a story…you've just read mine.

Our stories may be different and we may come from different lifestyles. Perhaps you have never been a drug addict or lesbian. Perhaps you didn't grow up in the projects, or you've never gone to jail. Yet there is one thing that is common to all of us: SIN.

Behold, I was shapen in iniquity,

and in sin did my mother conceive me.

Psalm 51:5

God views all sin the same. Without repentance, the liar, gossiper, adulterer, masturbator, fornicator and cheater will go to the same hell as the drug addict, homosexual, murderer, pedophile and thief.

Some may not believe in heaven or hell; bad or good; right or wrong. To each his own, only know that for every action there is a reaction. According to the Word of God, the Lord said, *Whatsoever is right I will pay.*

When the Word of Life was presented to me, first I had to acknowledge that my life was unmanageable (full of sin). Secondly, according to Psalm 51:1-5, and Romans 10:9-10, 13, I had to confess to God that I was a sinner and needed His help to stop practicing sin. That is the only way a person can be set free from power of sin. You cannot do it on your own.

Who Said It Couldn't Be Done?

To every person who holds this book of True Deliverance in your hands, please allow yourself to see yourself as you truly are, so that change might come your way. Then see yourself as God sees you: a sinner in need of forgiveness and total deliverance. I want you to know that the change in my life could not have happened unless and until I saw myself; then – and only then – was the Deliverance Power of God able to work in my life.

Again, I thank every reader who took time to read this awesome book of God's True Deliverance.

Written by Denise Jones M.S., B.A., CADC

Reference Page

Music Log

- Tex, Joe *I Gotcha*, 1967 ℗ 1991 Curb Records, Inc.
- The Clark Sisters, *I Can Do All Things Thru Christ That Strengthens Me*, Unworthy; 1976 (Lead: Karen Clark)
- Wilmington Chester Mass Choir, *Stand Still (Until His Will Is Clear)*, Recorded live at Fellowship Baptist Church, Chicago, Illinois, November 2, 1991
- Walter Hawkins & Love Center Choir, *Changed*, Love Alive © 1993 CGI
- Charles Nicks & Saint James Choir, *Come to Jesus*, Dearborn MI; Fort Auditorium, Detroit, MI.
- Cleophus Robinson GOSPSOUL: Cleophus Robinson & Sister Josephine James *Sweet Home* 1962
- Inez Andrew, *Lord Don't Move Mountain*, 1970
- Crouch, Andrae, *Through It All*, Word, 1970

Drug Log

- Heroin - opium
- Cocaine - upper
- Dilaudid - opium
- Talwin (T's) pain killer
- Pyribenzamine, (Blues) - antihistamine
- Ritalin – hyperactive children (ADD/ADHD)
- Tac or PCP (Phencyclidine), which is a hallucinogenic
- Locker-Room – Formaldehyde (embalming fluid)
- 529J, 591, wheel chairs - opium
- Placidyl – sleeping pill
- Cough syrup with codeine (Robitussin, Tussionex, P.Bur, Alnon, Gusteni)

Who Said It Couldn't Be Done?

Denise was born and reared in the midst of a drug-infested environment on Chicago's West Side. The oldest of seven siblings, Denise was reared by her grandmother in a sweet but bitter home. By the time, she was five; several family members had molested her. At the age of eleven, her mother introduced her to an environment overridden with drugs, sex and crime. Succumbing to the pressure of her environment, Denise began shooting heroin at age twelve, initiating a cycle of crime and addiction that lasted 14 years.

In 1986, Denise met the Lord Jesus Christ, who gave her a second chance at life and rewrote her destiny. Upon changing her lifestyle and connecting with positive people, Denise overcame the adversities controlling her life and has lived the last 24 years clean and sober. After years of drug abuse, she made the cognitive decision to turn her life around and do something positive for herself.

Denise is also a deliverance minister, author, and motivational speaker in and around the Chicago area. She has over 10 years' experience motivating small business owners, entrepreneurs and individuals to use their innate abilities to master and achieve their dreams and goals.

Who Said It Couldn't Be Done?

Denise's love and compassion for the disadvantaged has inspired her to write her first book, *"Who Said It Couldn't Be Done?"* This candid, true-life account is a heartwarming, inspirational story about a little girl whose mother failed her, and the emotional devastation encountered as a result of that failure. Denise's book is also about choices–good ones as well as bad ones.

The Author is making herself available to her audience. If there are any comments or questions, feel free to contact her at <u>authordenisejones@gmail.com</u> or by phone **708-932-6417**